*With appreciation for your support
as a Contributing Member of
the Smithsonian National Associate Program*

This drawing by the architect demonstrates the interrelationship of design motifs among the site's preexisting buildings and the new garden, pavilions, and kiosk.

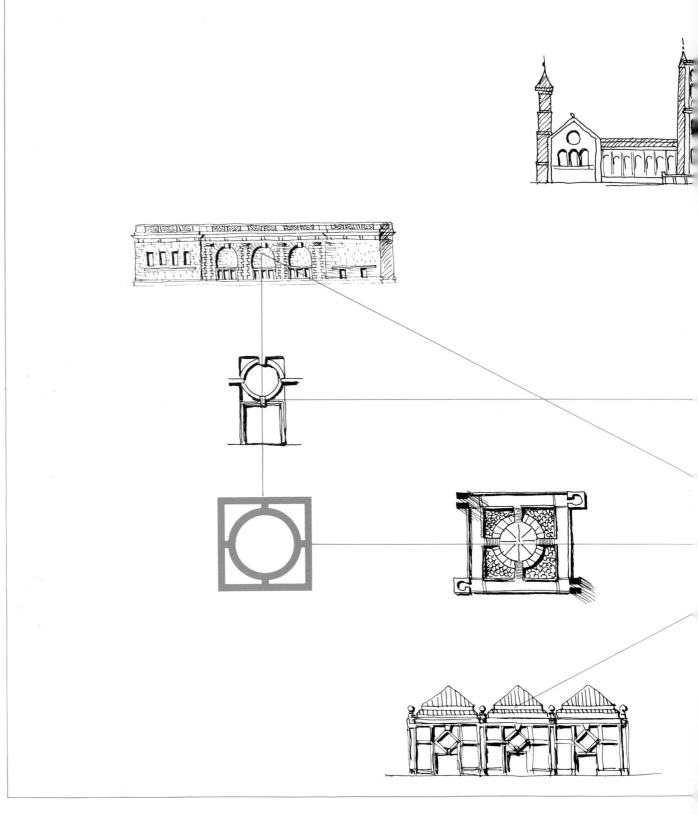

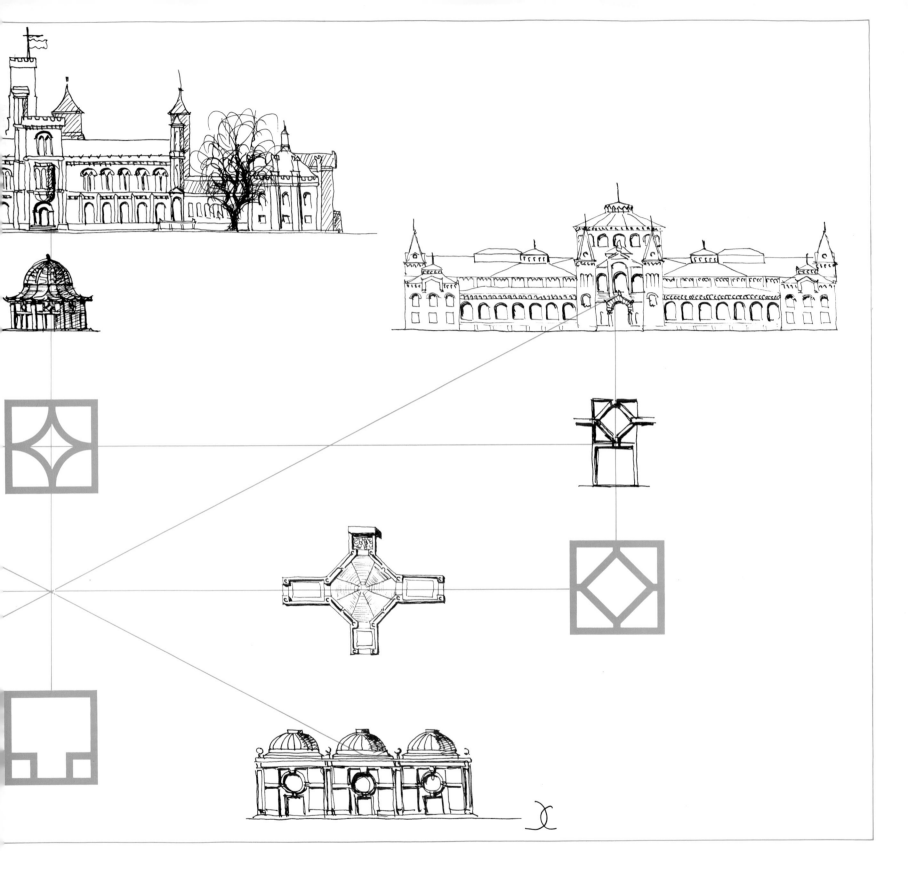

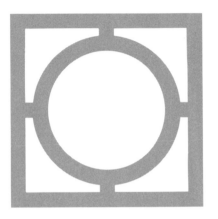

SMITHSONIAN INSTITUTION PRESS
WASHINGTON, D.C.
LONDON

A New View
from
the Castle

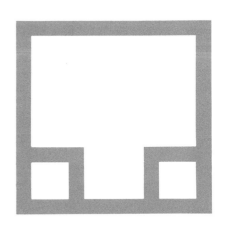

ARTHUR M. SACKLER GALLERY

NATIONAL MUSEUM OF AFRICAN ART

S. DILLON RIPLEY CENTER

ENID A. HAUPT GARDEN

EDWARDS PARK
AND
JEAN PAUL CARLHIAN

Acknowledgments

The editors wish to thank our colleagues in the Smithsonian Institution for counsel and support in project development: James Hobbins, Executive Assistant to the Secretary; James McK. Symington, Director of the Office of Membership and Development; Jeffrey LaRiche, Office of the Assistant Secretary for Public Service; Milo C. Beach, Assistant Director for the Arthur M. Sackler Gallery; Sylvia Williams, Director, National Museum of African Art; in the Office of Architectural History and Historic Preservation, Cynthia Field, Director, James Goode, former Keeper of the Smithsonian Institution Building, and Colin Varga; Madeleine Jacobs, Katherine Kirlin, Linda St. Thomas, and Lilas Wiltshire in the Office of Public Affairs; Carol Beehler, Kim Nielsen, and Susan Bliss, Sackler Gallery; Margaret Bertin, NMAfA; in the Office of Horticulture, Director James R. Buckler, Kathryn Meehan, and August Dietz IV; David Andrews, SITES; Joe Carper, SNAP, Kathryn Stafford, RAP; Kathy Dorman, Joseph Henry Papers; Susan Glenn, SI Archives; Jay Joyner, Freer Gallery; Frank C. Gilmore, Office of the Director of Facilities Services; Paul Rasmussen, Office of Design and Construction; and Bruce D. Smith, NMNH.

We were fortunate to have the guidance of our colleagues at the Smithsonian Institution Press. In the University Press we thank Alan Carter, Senior Designer, Ruth W. Spiegel, Senior Editor, and Jeanne Sexton, Editor. At Smithsonian Books we thank Alexis Doster III, Senior Editor, John F. Ross, Editor, and Frances C. Rowsell, Picture Editor.

Finally, we owe special thanks to Charles Putnam, Construction Engineer, General Services Administration, and Susan T. Steele, Director of Public Affairs, Shepley, Bulfinch, Richardson and Abbott.

Page 17: Staircase in African Pavilion. Pages 18-19: Sackler Pavilion and garden, at left; African Pavilion and garden, right; architectural features above. Pages 20-21: Staircases of Sackler Pavilion, at left, and African Pavilion, right, with architectural features of quadrangle buildings across top. Pages 22-23: South entrance to the Enid A. Haupt Garden through the Renwick Gates; page 23, African Pavilion and garden, center; detail of stained glass, above. Page 24: Sackler garden with moongate sculpture in front of Kiosk; Kiosk detail. Page 25: Moongate frames the Arts and Industries Building. Pages 26–27: Central Concourse of the S. Dillon Ripley Center with illusionist mural by Richard Haas, at right. Pages 28–29: Scenes of the Enid A. Haupt Garden. Pages 30–31: The quadrangle today and shortly before groundbreaking in 1983. Page 32: Smithsonian Castle overlooks the Victorian centerpiece of the Enid A. Haupt Garden.

Cover: Pavilion and Kiosk watercolors by Shu-xiang Xi, SBRA. Garden drawing, SBRA, adapted by Melody Sarecky.

The James Smithson Society of the Smithsonian Institution has provided generous support for this publication.

Staff for A New View from the Castle

Editorial Director/Concept — Maureen R. Jacoby
Editor-in-Chief — Michelle K. Smith
Designer — Lynne Komai/ The Watermark Design Office

Production Manager — Kathleen Brown
Copy Editor — Joan Holleman
Editorial Assistant — Jeanie J. Kim

Library of Congress Cataloging-in-Publication Data

Park, Edwards.
    A new view from the Castle.

    1. Carlhian, Jean Paul—Criticism and interpretation. 2. Shepley, Bulfinch, Richardson, and Abbott. 3. Arthur M. Sackler Gallery (Smithsonian Institution) 4. National Museum of African Art (U.S.) 5. S. Dillon Ripley Center (Smithsonian Institution) 6. Architecture, Modern—20th century—Washington (D.C.) 7. Washington (D.C.)—Buildings, structures, etc. 8. Enid A. Haupt Garden (Washington, D.C.) I. Carlhian, Jean Paul. II. Title. NA737.C26P37
1987   727'.7'0924   87-42555
ISBN 0-87474-749-X (pbk.)

British Library Cataloging-in-Publication Data is available.

The paper used in this publication meets the minimum requirements of the American National Standard for Permanence of Paper for Printed Library Materials Z39.48–1984.

C O N T E N T S

F O R E W O R D
Robert McC. Adams

In observing the throngs of daily visitors to Smithsonian museums here on the Mall, it has occurred to me that few are likely to be aware of the Institution's international origins. When British nobleman-scientist James Smithson died in Genoa, Italy, in 1829, the terms of his will revealed that a strange bequest might henceforth benefit the young United States of America. The childless Smithson stipulated that if his sole heir, a nephew in England, were to die without issue the full proceeds of his estate were to pass to the United States government "to found at Washington under the name of the Smithsonian Institution an Establishment for the increase and diffusion of knowledge among men." Little thought was given to exactly what that meant, but in 1835, when the nephew died, sans progeny, the Jackson administration and the twentieth congress began to wrestle with the interesting task of channeling the £105,000 they suddenly had to deal with into a fitting vehicle that would honor the terms of Smithson's will.

At almost precisely that same time a young Frenchman embarked on a journey to the new nation and recorded his impressions in a series of notebooks he kept while visiting centers of commerce and the western frontiers. Alexis de Tocqueville was twenty-five years old when he crossed the Atlantic in May 1831. The forces of the industrial revolution were under way in Europe as harbingers of enormous social, economic, and political change. Keenly astute and sensitive to the times, Tocqueville probed the essence of the American system of government and the character of the American people as counterparts to those conditions that he understood in France and Great Britain. In *Journey to America* he wrote, "However powerful and impetuous the course of history is here, imagination always goes in advance of it, and the picture is never large enough. There is not a country in the world where man more confidently takes charge of the future, or where he feels with more pride that he can fashion the universe to please himself. It is a movement of the mind which can only be compared with that which brought about the discovery of the New World three centuries ago."

Against this seething climate of expansion and intellectual growth, the Smithson bequest was formally accepted in 1836 and became a kind of political football in Congress and among the intelligentsia. For almost a decade the objectives were disputed and it was not until 1846 that various forces reconciled and the Smithsonian Institution was established. Its headquarters building, the Castle designed by architect James Renwick, Jr., rose on the Mall. Its form and function were subjected to further hearty disputes among those who saw the Smithson mandate as one for pure scientific research and those who would have it serve as a national library.

After mid-century, the Smithsonian became either a participant in or repository for specimens collected on a vast number of scientific expeditions, both domestic and foreign. It stood at the forefront of scientific inquiry into the flora and fauna of the western part of our continent. Thus developed the museum aspect of the Institution, always under the watchful eye of Congess, as its scientists amassed collections, studied them, and disseminated their findings in publications that established its identity in the international scientific community.

Its museum focus was more or less sealed when Congress decided that many of the objects displayed at the great Centennial Exposition in Philadelphia in 1876 were to be housed permanently in Washington under the beneficent wing of the Smithsonian. The first National Museum Building was erected next to the Castle and some forty trainloads of artifacts and manufactured objects from as far as the Phillippines and Japan and China joined displays of European and American manufacture. Although in the ensuing century the Victorian Arts and Industries Building has been used for other purposes, it is again the home for the centennial objects.

Smithson's bequest has continued to attract comparably generous gestures. In 1906 Detroit industrialist Charles Lang Freer deeded his astonishing collection of oriental antiquities to the nation and four years after his death in 1919, the Freer Gallery of Art opened, occupying the area directly west of the Castle.

Throughout the balance of the twentieth century, the Smithsonian has extended its international interests, engaging in regular scientific international exchange programs of scientific data and literature. Its staff conducts research on five continents. It is host to frequent international seminars and loan exhibitions from abroad.

As recently as 1979 the Smithsonian acquired, by act of Congress, the burgeoning young Museum of African Art, then occupying a succession of connected townhouses on Capitol Hill. The collection was founded in the 1960s by a devoted Africanist, Warren Robbins, who had been a foreign service officer and, although not a wealthy man, had amassed a formidable collection of representative African art objects.

Little wonder, then, as we approach a new century and consider marking the Quincentenary observance of Columbus's landing in the Americas, that the Smithsonian vision would seek a fitting expansion for activities and museum efforts that reflect its place in the world community.

The story of Dillon Ripley's concept for use of the quadrangle of land left on the Mall adjacent to the Castle, the Freer, and the Arts and Industries Building is recounted in these pages.

Here I would like to turn to my own experience over these past three years as Secretary of the Smithsonian to convey the enormous sense of excitement and fulfillment that has accompanied the completion of the building project. When I first occupied this office I could see from my window the construction site as it is described in the chapter on the Big Hole. That hole was indeed big, and it was muddy and seemingly chaotic. But from it has emerged a wondrous garden, really three gardens, and two entry pavilions, and a small domed structure that is called for some reason a Kiosk.

The saga of the garden is yours to read in this book, but it has been my privilege to come to know its benefactress, a woman whose sense of style and elegance has endowed all of us with a retreat that carries the themes of the collections that are displayed beneath it. The Enid A. Haupt Garden will stand for a long time as a tribute to the woman who shared the vision of creating a great garden on the Mall.

In bestowing a remarkable gift to the nation, the late Dr. Arthur M. Sackler has enabled the Smithsonian to achieve a position unique within the world's museum community. Complementing the Freer collection, the 1,000 masterworks of Asian and Near Eastern art given by Dr. Sackler constitute the opening exhibition for the new gallery bearing his name.

Early in the formulation of his participation in the quadrangle project, Dr. Sackler spoke feelingly of what he hoped the new museum complex would portray: "Culture is not just sculpture and painting. Culture is the whole range of man's creative sensibilities. What the quadrangle means to me is that we are recognizing ourselves as part of a total world—larger than that of a western world or of a European world—one which encompasses all continents. And so, over a span of twenty-five hundred years, an artist speaks to us today. And what we see is an emotional communication between the artist and us, over time and over space."

In its new home the National Museum of African Art may consolidate its holdings under one roof and display them in appropriate gallery space for the first time.

Recently museum director Sylvia Williams talked of the art she knows so well and about the new complex: "The traditional art of Africa has a remarkable energy—it is a language; it conveys ideas. The sculpture served for thousands of years as a primary means of communication between generations. These objects have been a principal carrier of basic knowledge like the silent, printed symbols on the pages of books. The quadrangle is absolutely unique. It's never been done before—on this scale, this dimension. It opens a whole new horizon on the continent of Africa and its art."

The International Center, appropriately housed in the S. Dillon Ripley Center, marks the beginning of a new generation of intercultural and interdisciplinary programs at the Smithsonian. Past Secretary Ripley observed, "For us in the West, it is now time to look beyond our immediate horizon. We need reminders of the two-thirds of the world that are not Western. . . . The quadrangle will emphasize the diversity and oneness of us as humans. I consider it the most significant project the Smithsonian has ever undertaken."

These random thoughts from some of the principals help convey some of that sense of excitement I mentioned earlier. We are witnesses to the culmination of dreams, the unique imagination that is American and that has inspired us for two hundred years.

Of that movement of the American mind that Tocqueville found so laudatory, he went on to say, ". . . one must not imagine that such thoughts only take place in a philosopher's head. . . . They belong to every object. They form a part of all feelings; they are palpable, visible, felt and, in some sort, strike all the senses."

We celebrate in this book the confluence of forces that has brought about the Institution's latest achievement—a grand complex of museums and spaces for educational pursuits that are palpable and strike the senses. That their embodiment was formulated by an expatriate Frenchman is oddly appropriate. Jean Paul Carlhian and his brilliant team of architects have created a remarkable underground world that is surely a fashioning of the universe to please, not only themselves, but a grateful nation. ∎

PREFACE
Edwards Park

Describing a building is a daunting prospect. A writer may wrench himself into the language of architects, and discuss pediments and entablatures and sexpartite vaults, or he can plunge uncomfortably into poesy, gasping at "cloud-capp'd towers," dreaming of dwelling in marble halls. I was fortunate enough to dodge both traps, for the Smithsonian's new museum and garden complex on its quadrangle is very much the story of people—idealists and realists, dreamers and doers, designers and users, builders and planters.

The drama that has been unfolding south of the Smithsonian Castle for so long—really a score of years—has a cast of at least hundreds. I was able to catch a few of the principals between acts, and test their good nature by probing at their expertise and their memories. Charles Putnam, construction engineer for the General Services Administration, patiently shepherded me through the construction site, again and again, explaining slurry walls and tiebacks, and saving me from being ground into the mud by trucks, or buried under a giant scoop of wet concrete.

Director of the Office of Horticulture James R. Buckler, who has worked devotedly to produce the new Enid A. Haupt Garden, gave me a memorable tour of his domain, the Smithsonian greenhouses, where the plants were being gathered. Former Smithsonian administrators Charles Blitzer and Paul Perrot recalled fascinating details of the quadrangle's origins. Peter Powers, the Smithsonian's General Counsel, augmented them.

Finally I was able to collar one of the busiest people on the Washington Mall, S. Dillon Ripley, Secretary Emeritus of the Institution, still working long hours and traveling incessantly, always with the ultimate good of the Smithsonian foremost in his mind. The quadrangle was his conception, his dream, one of his chief absorptions throughout his tenure. He raised millions of dollars for it. He battled Congress for it. He cajoled, jollied, begged, fumed, and shoved to get the job done. And at last it is.

My most constant source, however, was the chief architect of the quadrangle project, Jean Paul Carlhian, a principal in the Boston architectural firm of Shepley, Bulfinch, Richardson and Abbott. For months Jean Paul and I met regularly, donning hard hats at the construction site so we could explore the work in progress, then breaking for lunch and talk. Jean Paul explained the rationale of his design, interpreted his plans, and led me through the steps of their fulfillment. He accepted my presence in his office and introduced me to his design team. He took me into his home.

Inevitably, I slid into the role of a sort of Boswell: friend and confidante as well as reporter. I relished it, for this particular Johnson is very good copy. Carlhian is not only an experienced teacher of architecture, but an expressive, imaginative communicator. I'll admit now something that I would have stoutly denied a couple of years ago: he could have written this book himself. A great many of the words are his. Happily for me, he was too busy to take on the job.

My role as Carlhian-watcher helps explain the path this book follows, deviating from third person description to first person narrative, from cool appraisal to warm involvement. One cannot trail along behind a vibrant, loquacious, often amusing, sometimes bad tempered, always charming expert and remain meticulously aloof. He infected me with his enthusiasm and pride, his impatience and frustrations.

Together we watched the great quad structure grow within its deep excavation and crop out in two beautiful pavilions and a kiosk. And I began to glimpse the blossoming creation through his eyes—a mere, occasional flash of insight, but enough to stir me with understanding.

This story has grown with that understanding. But many times it might have wilted in its adolescence had it not been for Maureen Jacoby, Assistant Director and Managing Editor of Smithsonian Institution Press, and Michelle Smith, editor for this book. They refreshed me with their own eagerness, they restored my sometimes sunken spirits, they stroked my ego, and they literally nourished my collaboration with Jean Paul Carlhian by picking up the tabs (sometimes with a wince) for several productive luncheons. In short, they kept the faith. And they earned our lasting gratitude and affection.

This, then, is a book about a concept that became a design. It tells of themes and the reasons for them, of carefully deliberated subtleties of lighting, motifs, colors, and shapes. It explains the need for broad breathing spaces far underground. It describes the architectural task of serving an important purpose in a way that has not been tried before on such a scale. And it is a record of excellence—in deliberation, in planning, in materials and construction, in the cohesion of details that makes a design work.

It was quite impossible for me to remain a distant reporter during this task. Like it or not, I entered the narrative, and the quadrangle became my project, too. ∎

December 1983

December 1984

September 1983

August 1985

December 1986

"It will be more than a museum, more than an underground complex of steel and granite. It is an idea. An idea that has grown out of a single need—our need to know about art, cultures, and peoples that are beyond our immediate horizon, the great diversity of the non-Western world, the imagination and genius that are Africa, the Middle East, and Asia."

Thomas Lawton, Director, Arthur M. Sackler
Gallery and Freer Gallery of Art

One of the people who taught me a lot about life was a New England boat builder. He still built in wood, turning out twelve-foot racing dinghies that were a delight to sail, light and quick and handsome. But it was the building of them that fascinated me, for the whole process was based on *tension*.

My friend would shape the keel and the curved stem that rose from it at the bow. He'd steam the ribs and bend them up from the keel, and steam the gunwales and force them around the ribs. He'd hold this framework in place with long wooden clamps until he could bolt it down. Then he'd steam his planking and bend that around the ribs, and clamp each board until he'd set his screws and sunk them deep.

I'd watch him torture the wood and I could almost feel it straining to straighten out and return to mere lumber. But it couldn't. Every distorted element of it was held tight by another distorted factor. Keel, stem, transom, ribs, gunwales, planking, thwarts—all worked in opposition, each tense piece trapped into place by another, just as tense. I'd wonder why the unfinished vessel didn't explode—jagged splinters and bronze screws humming through the shop like shrapnel.

Instead, that tension produced an object of airy grace and symmetry, of fragile beauty yet enormous strength. The finished boat seemed almost alive, seeking its destiny afloat, dainty yet purposeful.

It took my old friend about three weeks in his lakeside New Hampshire shop to build a dinghy. It took seven years of excavation and construction along Washington's Independence Avenue to produce the great underground museum complex and research center that lies under the Smithsonian Institution's fabulous Enid A. Haupt Garden. Like those small boats, the vast structure within the Smithsonian's quadrangle grew from the interplay of tension, this time on a gigantic scale. And again the result is a breathtaking human accomplishment.

Visitors to the Smithsonian—over 20 million of them a year—pass through an orientation center in the old Castle, the original Smithsonian building on the National Mall. Here they learn, perhaps for the first time, exactly what this strange Institution is, what it offers—a unique under-

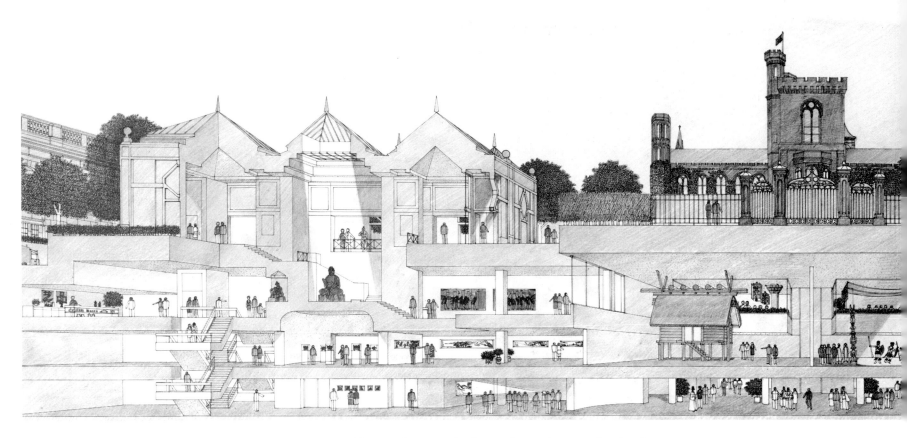

standing of the world around us—and what it demands: a good pair of legs, and the patience to learn from objects. The reception staff points out the various options that the Smithsonian's many establishments in and around Washington offer to sightseers. A film reinforces the briefing. Finally, casual visitors set their own courses for their pilgrimage.

Many are tempted to pass through the South Door of the Castle, for it swings open on an alluring world of blossoming plants and exotic foliage, of lawns and patterned shrubs, of walks and lampposts and benches. If you pass through that door, you face a parterre, spreading before you like a decorative carpet. Beyond it, directly in line with the door, stand the Renwick Gates, based on a design by James Renwick, Jr., the Castle's architect. The gates are handmade cast- and wrought-ironwork swinging from sandstone piers of the same reddish stone that went into the Castle's walls. On each side of the parterre the earth rises and falls in hills and valleys, ridges and embankments, all reduced to the scale of a garden. Here you come upon sudden decorative oases where you can sit and contemplate and perhaps hear the splashing of a tiny waterfall.

You also move, irresistibly, toward one or the other of the pavilions, alike yet not twins, that rise among the garden's trees and plants on each side of the center axis—South Door, through parterre, through Renwick Gates. The pavilion on the eastern side presents a sense of roundness. Its roof consists of six rounded copper domes; its facade features round arches

under each dome. The other pavilion, equidistant on the western side of the axis, is a match, but with angles instead of round arches. Its roof is six copper pyramids, its long facade is sculptured with three diamonds. Both pavilions fit into the garden's berms—those swelling hillocks and small vales—and seem smaller structures than they are.

These pavilions, ninety by sixty feet in area and about thirty-six feet high, are the entrances to the underground museum complex. The western one, nearest the Freer, leads to the Arthur M. Sackler Gallery, which houses the Sackler collection of Asian and Near Eastern art. The other, near the old Arts and Industries Building, takes you down to the National Museum of African Art. Both greet the visitor with a long, impressive room that subtly carries on the motif of its roof and windows, round or diamond shaped. Ceiling beams and floor paving in each pavilion reflect its particular theme. So do the frames of the northern windows that look out on the garden. Opposite these windows, a stairwell in each structure contains a grand flight of stairs, flooded with brightness from a skylight above and a window in the south wall.

In the African Pavilion, soft colors glow in the ceiling. In both pavilions, the floors are pinkish granite. All the metal—window sashes, handrail fittings—is blue-green, flecked with gold. The off-white walls edge toward beige.

In each pavilion, you pass the length of this long room before turning,

■ *In 1981 this cross-section rendered by the firm of Shepley, Bulfinch, Richardson and Abbott set forth the imagined inner workings of the quadrangle project. Over the years so much has changed or been altered that it bears little resemblance to the final building opening to the public in September 1987.*

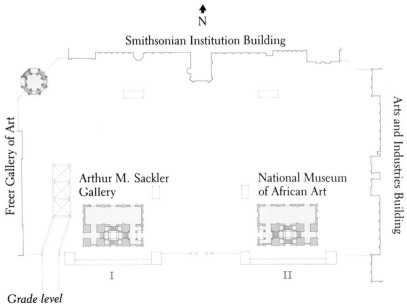

N

Smithsonian Institution Building

Freer Gallery of Art

Arthur M. Sackler Gallery

National Museum of African Art

Arts and Industries Building

I

II

Grade level

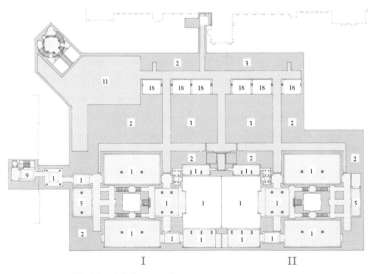

I

II

First level below grade

leaving your coat at a checkroom, and facing a broad staircase. All your life you've been accustomed to *climbing* stairs in order to reach splendid places—Mont-Saint-Michel, Edinburgh Castle, the Sydney Opera House, the United States Capitol, and also eight Smithsonian museums right here on the Mall.

Now you are beckoned *downward* by this grand stairway. It is broad and impressive, and splits around its stairwell so that you can look down over the polished bronze handrail and see, three stories below, the still surface of a pool, reflecting the daylight that floods downward from the skylit cupola, far above. In the western pavilion, leading to the Arthur M. Sackler Gallery, the stairway angles right and left so that in plan it forms the diamond motif of the building. And the pool at the bottom, too, forms a gleaming diamond. The counterpart stairwell down to the National Museum of African Art repeats the round motif. It is circular in plan, descending to a circular reflecting pool.

As you reach the first level and leave the stairway, you find the subtle intellectual impact of the architecture, the repeated statement of themes, the sense of daylight and color and splendor toned down to allow the museum treasures full play. You find yourself in a square foyer bounded by four round columns—an entrance gallery. On each side other galleries, carpeted to still your footsteps, await you.

Before exploring the galleries you move forward toward the Great Hall, the central exhibition area, designed for the ages as an enormous open space, without columns, two full stories in height, nearly ten thousand square feet in area. In the African museum, half of the designed hall—still a vast space—exists, and draws you immediately to it. From balconies you can look down on the great interior courtyard, conceived as an exhibition hall for special displays and events. In the Sackler, however, the jewel-like size of many pieces requires smaller, more intimate spaces. So the museum makes use of its part of the Great Hall by putting in a

1 *Exhibition*
2 *Exhibition support*
3 *Collection support*
4 *General support*
5 *Museum shop*
6 *Education*
7 *Research*
8 *Administration*
9 *Freer connection*
10 *SI Building connection*
11 *Truck ramp and loading dock*
12 *Education Center*
13 *Education Center auditorium*
14 *National Associate Program*
15 *Resident Associate Program*
16 *International Center*
17 *SITES*
18 *Concourse*
19 *Mechanical*

■*Looking south from the Castle, the moongate garden leads to the Arthur M. Sackler Gallery, left; above, a street scene ninety feet below the surface; below, the floor plans.*

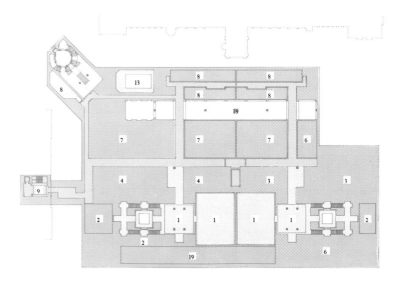

Second level below grade

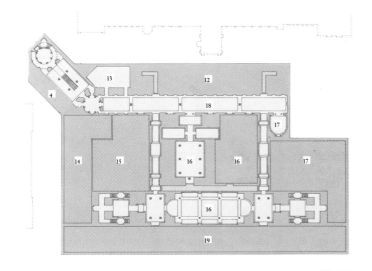

Third level below grade

second story and subdividing into smaller exhibit rooms. The spaces here are elastic. Walls can be removed for special exhibits.

This alteration to the accepted design was not achieved without controversy, for it meant that the structure would lose its perfect symmetry, and that the tremendous impact of huge openness, so far underground, would be sacrificed. On the other hand, the purpose of both museums was to display priceless exhibits in the most effective way. As in building a boat, tension between design and usage produced a special result. On the African side, where many exhibits are large, that splendid architectural breathing space works, so half of it is retained. In the Sackler, the glittering wealth of finger-size items is itself breathtaking, and the architecture has been muted.

Descending the stairs to the second level, you can, in each museum, turn back through the naturally lit stairwell and cross it, one floor above the pools. Again you face an entrance gallery and from it, on the African side, you may enter the Great Hall. That beautiful space and the galleries that now fill it in the Sackler furnish the only museum areas on this second level. The rest of this floor is occupied by offices, other museum uses, and plenty of that cherished Smithsonian commodity, storage space.

Descend again, circling the reflecting pool at the bottom of your stairwell. Tiles gleam beneath the still water. In the diamond-shaped pool of the Sackler, the tiles are jade green; in the round African pool they are blue.

The third level, known as the S. Dillon Ripley Center, is given over to more offices and special-purpose rooms of the Education Center, except directly under the Great Hall. Here, occupying its full designed dimensions—116 by 78 feet—is the International Gallery, the exhibition hall of the International Center. You are drawn in by special programs and displays, aimed at continuing the historic use of the Smithsonian as an agency to foster understanding between nations. The Center's offices and conference rooms are located between the Gallery and the Concourse.

As the pavilion stairways link the entrances with the museums' underground exhibition areas, corridors on the first and second levels link the exhibition areas of the complex, on its southern side, to the museums' office and support areas that run along beside the south facade of the Castle—or rather, beside its foundations, far underground. The S. Dillon Ripley Center has its own entrance for staff and the public attending exhibitions, classes, lectures, and workshops. This entrance is a circular off-white structure, forty-two feet in diameter, in the northwest corner of the Enid A. Haupt Garden. This structure looks like an old-fashioned bandstand, except that it is limestone instead of wooden "gingerbread." It is a kiosk, and that's exactly what it is called.

The Kiosk's round walls, widely windowed, bring abundant light inside. A circular staircase, along with the inevitable elevator, brings people down below. At the first level they meet a long escalator that carries them down the next two floors. On the third level the escalator deposits its passengers

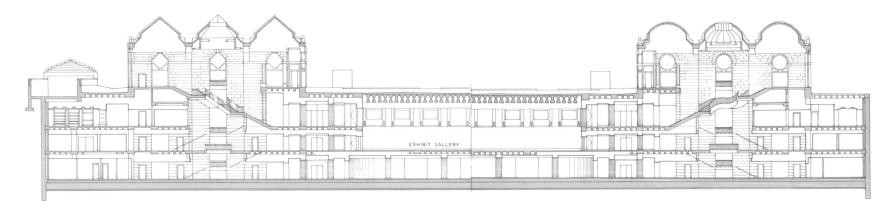

■ *By 1984 when this north elevation, above, was published by the* Architectural Record, *rooflines and staircase treatments had been refined. Opposite, the pavilion staircases.*

before a dark rotunda where deep green columns stand in silhouette against brightly lit brown walls.

This is a deliberately somber entranceway. It serves to turn you toward light, and when you step out of it (in about five steps; the rotunda isn't very big) you catch your breath at the contrast. For now, abruptly, you feel you are part of a street scene. So bright and airy are your surroundings that you feel you have walked outside.

Elegant doors in walls painted in blues, grays, and greens open onto the pavement. Upper-floor windows look down on you and you picture dawdling staff members leaning out to exchange office gossip with their neighbors. Six "garden spots" grow from evenly spaced planters, a fountain splashes in the center of the "street," and bountiful light streams down from four square skylights, each more than nine feet on a side.

This is called the Concourse, and it is lined by offices, labs, classrooms, and the auditorium of the Education Center. Two glass-walled bridges cross it on the second level, each an underground bridge of sighs. Four matching offices, also with glass walls, look down on the Concourse. These are for the directors and assistant directors of the African and Sackler museums. The office suites are exclusive, but also attractively warmed by the greenery in their long window boxes.

The Concourse is 285 feet long, extending the length of the building. Strolling eastward along it, you come face to face with the mural that has intrigued you since your first glimpse of it. Richard Haas's extraordinary *trompe l'oeil* reminds you that you are not on a street at all, but far below the towers and crenelations of the Castle, the spires and clerestory windows of the Arts and Industries Building. There they are in the mural, rising before your eyes against the sky. You feel you need only pass beneath that archway and . . .

. . . and you'll smack into the solid wall.

You're underground, all right. This entire structure, more than four acres in extent, is hidden from view under the rich soil of the Haupt Garden. It's buried treasure—priceless works of art and unique cultural and educational events within an intricate, endlessly rewarding complex of halls, galleries, and wonderful spaces in which to become happily lost in the best tradition of the Smithsonian. ■

Those of us who were on the Smithsonian staff in the 1970s will always think of S. Dillon Ripley when we visit the new museum complex. He explained to us back then the earliest plans for this strange, impressive underground center, and we listened skeptically to his far-reaching vision and blamed him for taking away "our" beautiful Victorian Garden. But did the first faint concept of transforming the Smithsonian's quadrangle come from this extraordinary man? Soon after entering upon this biography of the project, I decided to find out—from two of his assistant secretaries and from Mr. Ripley himself.

Secretary-Emeritus Ripley wasn't easy to find. Far from basking in retirement, he had been traveling steadily, continuing his ornithological research as well as fulfilling his commitments to various foundations and acting as goodwill ambassador for the Smithsonian. When I found him

Smithsonian buildings line the National Mall. U.S. Capitol at top; beginning of quadrangle construction at bottom right. Right, S. Dillon Ripley addresses guests at quadrangle groundbreaking, June 21, 1983.

in his big, sprawling office in the National Museum of Natural History, he was weary from the last trip and frantically busy preparing for the next. Typically, he put the press of time aside and gave himself completely to conversation with me. No sudden interruptions by jangling phones or surreptitious nods to messages signaled from the next room. Just courteous attention and careful answers to what must have seemed some pretty dumb questions about the origins of the quadrangle project.

Soon after he became Secretary of the Smithsonian in 1964, Mr. Ripley (he never used "Doctor") really began to appreciate the Mall. Whenever he left his office in the Castle he walked either beside or across it. The Mall entranced him, as it does everyone, a green spread of parkland, here flanked by Smithsonian buildings, with the splendid facade of the United States Capitol exquisitely etched at one end and the Washington Monument soaring skyward at the other. Mr. Ripley absorbed the grandeur of the setting and pondered its significance.

"Here was the place, it seemed to me, to help solve a great human problem, that of getting to *know* you. Here millions of Americans could come and get to know people from all over the world. Ordinarily, we never seem to be able to do that. When we go on a tour or a business trip, we always seem to be effectively isolated from the everyday people of our host country. But the Mall is our own 'turf,' and our Smithsonian museums certainly attract thousands of visitors from foreign lands."

He put the tips of his long fingers carefully together, thoughtfully. "When I was a child and first traveled with my family, I was deeply impressed by my mother suddenly remembering she had a cousin in Bombay. Since then I've always liked the idea of being at home anywhere, of being able to say, 'I have a dentist in Calcutta,' or simply, 'I know a family from West Germany.' And so, after I came to the Smithsonian in 1964, one of the first things I thought of was a sort of international center, a place on the Mall where people from other countries could forgather and hobnob with each other, and with Americans. Here the businessman from West Germany might discover that he had a friend or two in Washington. And here Americans would find other cultures comfortable, and not feel that they were 'amid the alien corn.' Obviously, the Smithsonian itself should be such a place."

Such thoughts prompted Ripley to make three notable gestures after he started his term as Secretary. One was to turn the statue of Joseph Henry around. For years the bronze likeness of the Institution's first Secretary had faced inward upon the Castle. Now, suddenly, it faced the Mall, and all the people thereon. "Come in and visit us," it said. "We belong to you."

Another was the dusting of the giant African elephant that stands, trunk raised, in the rotunda of the National Museum of Natural History. Ripley remembers with some amusement that some museum officials muttered that dusting off the elephant was sacrilegious. "One complained that it was historic dust," he recalled. But they obeyed the order, and so started

First Secretary of the Smithsonian Joseph Henry welcomes visitors at the Castle's Mall entrance, below; right, recent Folklife Festival celebrates India. Opposite, an annual Washington spring rite, the Kite Festival on the Mall draws kite fanciers of all ages.

a general sprucing up of the old exhibits in order to lure visitors.

And in 1967, Ripley inaugurated the Smithsonian Festival of American Folklife. Now, every summer, people from other lands, other cultures gather on the Mall and display their life styles—their songs, dances, cooking, crafts—and onlookers realize that they are learning more about, say, Peru, than they ever thought they'd know.

Dillon Ripley was by no means the first Secretary to reach out to people. His predecessor, Secretary Leonard Carmichael, supervised the building of the magnificent National Museum of American History and saw to it that exhibits were innovative and popular as well as scholarly. He was a strong supporter of the Smithsonian Institution Traveling Exhibition Service (SITES), one of the first true "outreach" programs of the old museum complex. And in the 1920s, Secretary Charles Doolittle Walcott recognized that the days when the Institution was solely for research were gone. Huge collections already crammed every corner of the existing buildings. People, ordinary people who walked along the Mall, were deeply and irrevocably involved with the place where their national treasures were stored and displayed. So Walcott proposed a "society of friends," to draw people into the Smithsonian family, but died before he could see his plan through.

Dillon Ripley raised the concept of outreach to new heights. He founded the Resident Associate Program in 1965 to encourage citizen participation in programs and special courses based on Smithsonian research. The Resident Associates were necessarily from in or around Washington, D.C. But after Ripley founded *Smithsonian* magazine in 1970, the Associate program went national. Regional programs of the Smithsonian National Associates brought Smithsonian experts and treasures to communities all over the world. An Associate was, in Ripley's words, "part of a vigorous educational and cultural force everywhere in the land."

But with his long background of travel, he was still haunted by the need to use the Institution as a base that foreign visitors could touch on occasion, where they would find some of the familiar tangibles of their homelands.

"Do you realize that so many of the embassies here in Washington are really islands of foreign culture that Americans can never visit? And they don't know us any better than we know them. Oman is an example of that isolation. A few years ago we had an Omani exhibition—you remember—partly because I'd gotten to know the Omani Embassy people here. We asked for some of their things and we displayed them at the Castle. And they were so excited. They'd never done this before in Washington. Here they were, actually meeting some ordinary American people—and vice versa.

"Of course, I'd always thought that an interplay of cultures was a common denominator of all the Smithsonian museums. It was one thing the Institution was all about. It had never occurred to me that museums were simply static collections. To me they were always supposed to be

lively, enjoyable adjuncts to learning—the way I found them when I traveled in Europe as a child."

Joseph Henry, 140 years ago, did not think of collections at all. He thought of the word "Institution" in the scholarly rather than social sense, and saw the new, uncertain establishment eventually becoming a campus—a cloister, perhaps—for scientists and researchers. It was Henry's successor, Secretary Spencer Fullerton Baird, who believed in the importance of collections and built up the museum concept at the Smithsonian. And what of S. Dillon Ripley, the eighth Secretary?

Paul Perrot, Ripley's Assistant Secretary for Museum Programs, says "Dillon saw objects as fundamental to the Smithsonian, but with scholarship as an accompaniment. He had a sort of vision in his head of an actual place within the Smithsonian where people could meet, a place to shield the Castle from Independence Avenue and complete the quadrangle. A place for contemplation? A library? Perhaps just a wall? Or better yet, a garden. . . ."

■ To clear the ground for construction, workmen pack up the Leonard Baskin sculpture of Spencer Fullerton Baird.

44

When funds were available, at the time of the nation's Bicentennial, Ripley decided on a Victorian garden to supplement the "Centennial of a Centennial" theme of the Arts and Industries Building. James R. Buckler, hired in 1972 to be Director of the Office of Horticulture, the first horticulturist ever at the Smithsonian, was given the assignment. From 1972 to 1976 Buckler completed in-depth research on the 1876 Centennial Exposition in Philadelphia and in particular the renowned Horticultural Hall, opened May 10, 1876, with its elaborate sunken embroidery parterre, cast-iron garden furniture, and displays of exotic tropical plants. Buckler's work was central to the design of the Smithsonian's Victorian Garden, but he recalled the Secretary's warning to him: "Don't get too fond of it. It won't stay forever." That was one of the most positive indications anyone had that the Victorian Garden wasn't enough. The Secretary had in his head vast plans for that meeting place that would complete the quadrangle.

According to Smithsonian General Counsel Peter Powers, since the mid-1960s Ripley had also considered providing new space in an above-ground building south of the Castle for the Freer Gallery and the Woodrow Wilson International Center for Scholars. The Wilson Fellows had been established by Congress in 1968 and housed in the Castle since 1970. This idea, in time, was discarded in favor of the notion to keep the Wilson Fellows in the Castle but expand the Freer by going underground.

Planning for the Freer involved some unusual considerations. Charles Lang Freer, in leaving his collection to the Smithsonian, did so under terms that have since become controversial. Freer's bequest prohibited the loaning or selling of any of his collection, and loans and exchanges are two important ways in which museums spread their wealth of learning.

But the Freer excels in research, publication, and other forms of scholarly exchange and does not bar the acquisition of more items. "The collection's about ten times the size it was in 1906, the time of the original deed of gift," Powers told me. Thus, although plans would change and develop, by the 1970s, providing more space for Asian and Near Eastern art was a fixed ingredient in the mix of reasons for completing the quadrangle.

More flavoring was added: architect James Renwick, Jr., it appeared, had in the mid-nineteenth century designed gates for the Castle, to be made of the same sandstone that went into the building's great reddish walls. The quarry that produced this stone hadn't moved an inch since it ceased operations in 1923. There it still was, beside the Potomac River, twenty-three miles upstream from Washington, at Seneca, Maryland, overgrown now, and well populated with copperheads, but still rich with sandstone. Unfortunately, however, the quarry falls within the National Historic Park that preserves and maintains the Chesapeake and Ohio Canal. Quarrying is no longer allowed.

In 1979 Mr. Ripley enlisted the aid of James Goode, keeper of the Smithsonian Institution Building (the Castle), to supervise the design and

■ *Two beloved features of the Victorian Garden were its central parterre and a giant European linden tree. The quadrangle's new garden took shape around these features.*

■*James Renwick, Jr., planned a southern gateway to Smithsonian grounds "planted with trees and shrubs, comprising about a hundred and fifty species, chiefly American"; above, James Goode is flanked by John Blake Murphy, left, who rendered the design, and Constantin Seferlis, who carved the stone.*

construction of the gates. Goode's first problem was finding the stone to build the gate piers.

He discovered that a number of huge, ancient boulders lay tumbled about the Seneca quarry. The same reddish sandstone. Just right for the gates. The National Park Service gave the Smithsonian special permission to snake out enough of these for the four piers of what are now called the Renwick Gates, opening onto the new Enid A. Haupt Garden.

James Goode arranged to have a full-size mock-up of the gates placed in the Victorian Garden so that Mr. Ripley and the assistant secretaries could see how they would look. They looked fine, but made the garden lovers uneasy, for they sensed something was going to happen to their favorite place.

It was typical of Ripley to move fast once the need for the new structure was well established. Paul Perrot recalled that Ripley learned of Junzo Yoshimura, the famous Japanese architect, through a family connection. The idea of an oriental touch for that still misty concept of a new building

■ *Architect's detailed plans, below, are implemented by workers, left.*

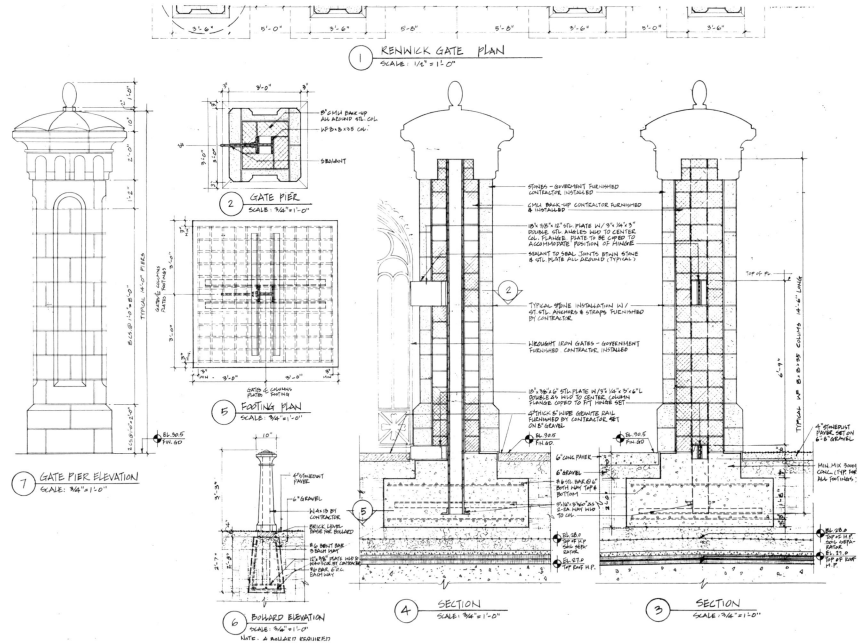

① RENWICK GATE PLAN
SCALE: 1½" = 1'-0"

② GATE PIER
SCALE: 3/4" = 1'-0"

8" CMU BACK-UP ALL AROUND STL. COL.
WF8×8×35 COL.
SEALANT

⑤ FOOTING PLAN
SCALE: 3/4" = 1'-0"

GATES & COLUMNS PLATES FOOTING

⑦ GATE PIER ELEVATION
SCALE: 3/4" = 1'-0"

⑥ BOLLARD ELEVATION
SCALE: 3/16" = 1'-0"
NOTE: 4 BOLLARD REQUIRED

4" STONEDUST PAVER
6" GRAVEL
W4×13 BY CONTRACTOR
BRICK LEVEL BASE FOR BOLLARD
#6 BENT BAR 3 EACH WAY
12"×3/8" PLATE WLD WITH 3 COL BY CONTRACTOR
#6 BAR 6" O.C. EACH WAY

STONES - GOVERMENT FURNISHED CONTRACTOR INSTALLED
CMU BACK-UP CONTRACTOR FURNISHED & INSTALLED
18"× 3/8"× 12" STL. PLATE W/ 3"× ¼"× 3" DOUBLE STL. ANGLES WLD TO CENTER COL. FLANGE. PLATE TO BE COPED TO ACCOMMODATE POSITION OF HINGE
SEALANT TO SEAL JOINTS BTWN STONE & STL. PLATE ALL AROUND (TYPICAL)
TYPICAL STONE INSTALLATION W/ ST. STL. ANCHORS & STRAPS FURNISHED BY CONTRACTOR
WROUGHT IRON GATES - GOVERNMENT FURNISHED. CONTRACTOR INSTALLED
18"× 3/8"× 6" STL. PLATE W/ 3"× ¼"× 3"× 6"L DOUBLE LS WLD TO CENTER COLUMN FLANGE COPED TO FIT HINGE SET
4" THICK 5" WIDE GRANITE RAIL FURNISHED BY CONTRACTOR SET ON 6" GRAVEL

TOP OF PL
TYPICAL WF 8×8×35 COLUMN 14'-6" LONG

EL. 30.5 FIN. GD.
6" CONC PAVER
6" GRAVEL
#6 STL BAR 6" BOTH WAY TOP & BOTTOM
3"× ¼"× 3"× 60" LS 2-EA WAY WLD TO COL.
EL. 28.0 TOP OF H.P SOIL SEPARATOR
EL. 27.0 TOP ROOF H.P.

EL. 30.5 FIN. GD.
4" STONEDUST PAVER SET ON 6"-8" GRAVEL
MIN. MIX 3000# CONC. (TYP. FOR ALL FOOTINGS)
EL. 28.0 TOP OF H.P. SOIL SEPARATOR
EL. 27.0 TOP OF ROOF H.P.

④ SECTION
SCALE: 3/4" = 1'-0"

③ SECTION
SCALE: 3/4" = 1'-0"

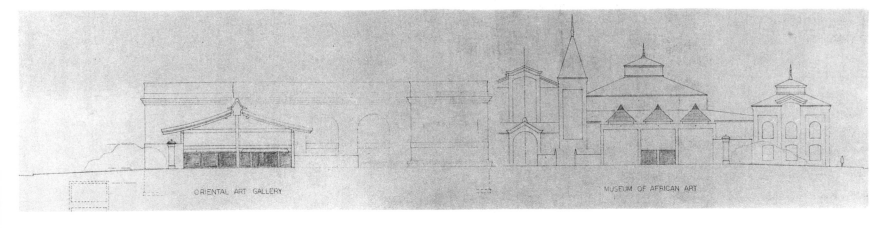

ORIENTAL ART GALLERY   MUSEUM OF AFRICAN ART

■ *First home of the National Museum of African Art was this Capitol Hill house, above, owned by black leader Frederick Douglass. Center, Yoshimura's earliest planning emphasizes indigenous architectural forms.*

renewed his thoughts about giving more space to Asian and Near Eastern art. Yoshimura's plans were most interesting. The mist started to blow away.

The desperate need of the National Museum of African Art to stretch out of the confining row houses it occupied on Capitol Hill added impetus, and Ripley also felt it was essential to emphasize African art and culture in the Smithsonian. Why not bring African art to the National Mall and build its new home on the quadrangle? Why not consider the new space a center where Americans could see for themselves the fascinating cultures of the two-thirds of the world that are not Western? Why not bring these cultures to the Smithsonian with a beautiful and impressive structure? Ripley found that his early dreams were beginning to take a firmer shape.

Finally the Arthur M. Sackler collection of Asian and Near Eastern art became available. Mr. Ripley put to work his special talent for inspiring in Dr. Sackler a sudden, strong interest in the Smithsonian. Here, of course, would be the perfect site for a *new* museum, an ideal home for the Sackler collection, would it not? Dr. Sackler, who would not live to see his gift completed, agreed wholeheartedly.

And so, abruptly, the plans came together. A new museum complex was necessary. And, happily, it would serve to complete the quadrangle, to block the view of the new and unwelcome Forrestal Building, and to provide a home for two museums, the Arthur M. Sackler Gallery and the National Museum of African Art. Finally, in the form of the S. Dillon Ripley Center, it would provide an actual place for the vision that had inspired Ripley for so many years. It would be a place where, as he said to me, there would be a "wonderful theater of operations" for research, exhibitions, and scholarly and public symposia.

So the quadrangle project simply follows the gradual, inevitable—and some say overdue—democratizing of the Smithsonian. Using *Smithsonian* magazine as his sounding board, Ripley has often explained his feelings about the great new museum complex:

"By creating such a 'window on the Mall,' the Smithsonian has a unique opportunity in these troubled times to reinvigorate its mandate 'for the increase and diffusion of knowledge among men.' Nearly 140

nations will have a theater of action here to exhibit, to express their cultural histories and their creation of much of the roots of our own civilization. . . . If anyone can create what can be a powerful force for understanding and for peace—the Smithsonian can—and must."

The rest of the story is history. The Yoshimura plan was right on track, but the Japanese architect suffered a stroke and a new architect was needed. The project had to receive the blessings of Congress. Once that was achieved, the Smithsonian asked the General Services Administration to act as general contractor. And the GSA requires open competition for all public projects. So bids went out to American architectural firms and, in Perrot's words, "mountains of credentials piled up on our desks."

From these, a handful of proposals emerged. And the great dream would be lived out. ■

■ *Left, the late Dr. Arthur M. Sackler, at right, joins Secretary Ripley at the presentation of his gift of one thousand works of Asian art. Below, this plan by Yoshimura retained the parterre and linden and featured sunken courtyards behind the pavilions.*

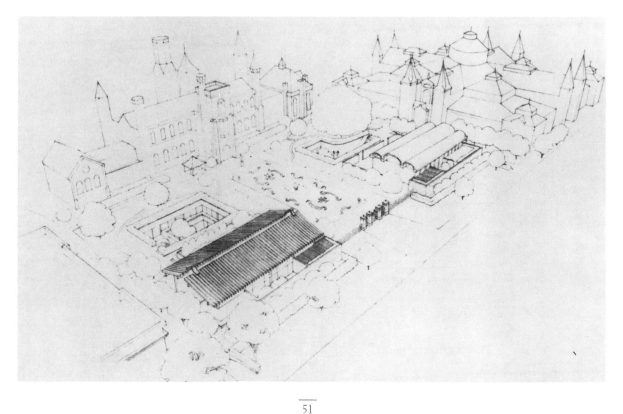

THE FIRM
Shepley, Bulfinch, Richardson and Abbott

An unobtrusive but carefully read newsletter, the *Commerce Business Daily*, circulates regularly around architectural firms. It describes upcoming federal building projects, chances for the right firm to try for a contract. On a bright Boston morning in November 1979, such a newssheet rotated around the executive desks of Shepley, Bulfinch, Richardson and Abbott (SBRA), whose offices occupy a fine neoclassical building (designed by the firm itself) in the shadowy maze of the old city's downtown business section.

The circular contained a description of a vast Washington project, an underground museum-and-study complex at the Smithsonian Institution. The write-up caught the eye of a principal, Jean Paul Carlhian, a brilliant Beaux Arts-trained French architect who had been assistant to the great Walter Gropius at Harvard before the oldest continuously operating architectural firm in the United States invited him to cross the Charles River and join them. Carlhian added his academic zeal to the firm—he had loved being on the Harvard faculty—and his knowledge of the requirements of university buildings and facilities. After coming to SBRA

■ *The reception area of the Boston offices of Shepley, Bulfinch, Richardson and Abbott, within a building they designed in 1923. Below, the staff in 1886.*

he designed three Harvard dormitories and other academic and cultural structures. Now the Smithsonian proposal intrigued him and he took it for discussion to the other principals at SBRA.

The old firm welcomes visitors and possible clients in a small, classically tasteful rotunda on the sixth floor of its building on Broad Street. Around the base of the domed ceiling appear the various names of the firm since its founding by the great Henry Hobson Richardson, father of America's Romanesque Revival. This discreet and tasteful display offers a gentle reminder of the firm's history, and helps explain whatever conservatism may surface among its top echelon: "H. H. Richardson—1874–1886," reads the circular list, and then continues: "Shepley, Rutan and Coolidge— 1886–1915; Coolidge and Shattuck—1915–1924; Coolidge, Shepley, Bulfinch and Abbott—1924–1952; Shepley, Bulfinch, Richardson and Abbott, 1952–" . . . a proud record of old New England names devoting themselves to the traditional New England work ethic with long and devoted service.

A project for the Smithsonian certainly seemed to be well within that tradition. After all, the firm had worked in Washington and even farther afield in the past, and recently had designed a number of museums. But since an unnamed designer was already involved in the project, the principals were reluctant to pursue it—with a designer on board, how could they avoid either relinquishing too much design control or stepping on his toes?

Jean Paul Carlhian pointed out that there was something special about a project on Washington's National Mall, right in the heart of the capital of the free world, and that the prestigious Smithsonian Institution would surely prove to be a unique client.

Moreover, the challenge of the proposal was hard to resist. Museums fascinate architects. And this complex involved problems that would try the souls of Sir Christopher Wren and Frank Lloyd Wright combined, not to mention H. H. Richardson himself. Let's give it a shot, said Carlhian. We can withdraw if we don't like it.

■ *Henry Hobson Richardson in his library, left; the workroom in 1886, below. An architectural conference, right.*

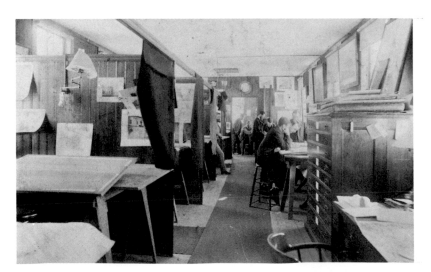

Well . . . said the other principals. The firm dispatched a proposal to the Smithsonian and assigned a team to the project, with Jean Paul Carlhian as its design leader. It was one of many that the Institution received, and it was one of the six that were chosen for further consideration. Along with the Smithsonian's request for an interview, the team received sketches of the existing concept. The architect responsible for the sketches was still unnamed, but Jean Paul liked his idea of an underground museum and its aboveground axial organization. He was less sure about the ethnic "statement," as architects call it, of the pavilions.

Three of the firm's best people flew down to Washington for the vital interview. Principal-in-charge Richard Potter led the task force, which included consulting engineers. Design principal Carlhian presented the new design approach. They faced an imposing jury, for it seems that just about every government and private environmental agency in Washington gets involved in a new building project, and now the General Services Administration brought together all of these questions and doubts. The SBRA team had to give satisfactory testimony about such problems as how to dig down sixty feet without imparting the slightest tremor to the precious walls of the Smithsonian Castle, only a few feet away.

"The interview lasted about an hour," project architect Robert Holloran recalls. "Then we were dismissed, and another firm went in to face the music. We piled into taxis and went over to Washington National Airport to fly back to Boston on the six o'clock plane. We were all on board, fastening our seat belts, when the stewardess came by with a message for Mr. Potter. He got to a telephone, and then came back and yelled, 'We got the job!' " With that, Potter scrambled off the plane at the last minute, and hurried back to the Smithsonian to go over the contract.

Not until then did the Institution reveal the name of the original architect, Junzo Yoshimura. "He came to my home in Concord," Carlhian recalls. "I took him into my work room, where no one is allowed without my invitation. My books were stacked all over the floor as they always are, and my papers were spread out on my big table, and Junzo said, 'At last! A room exactly like mine!' Of course I instantly became fond of him."

SBRA's team came up with fresh design concepts and produced drawings to illustrate them. They kept the original idea of aboveground pavilions, but these went through a series of transformations because of gradual changes in the Smithsonian's requirements, as well as those of the various review bodies that oversee Washington buildings.

With the job in hand, the Boston team expanded in size, assigning capable hands to every detail. Schematics had to be drawn and the budget planned before a start could be made on the working drawings. "These are what the contractors bid on," says Holloran. "Architects have to explain every nut and bolt so the builders know exactly what their costs will be."

And so the work started—years of intensive and often frustrating effort.

"Most clients don't check every architectural step," Holloran points out. "But Smithsonian people are different. Ever curator made it clear to us that his own gallery was the most important one in the building."

Project designer Carlhian had to interrupt his creative work with some high-voltage Washington meetings. One of the first was with Smithsonian Secretary S. Dillon Ripley. "I was terrified," he says. "There were all the assistant secretaries at the conference table, and there was one empty chair: Ripley's. Everyone sat quietly until he showed up."

Carlhian had brought some ideas to show, and being an enthusiast, he got excited about what he was saying to these highly important Smithsonian personages. When the meeting was over, one of Ripley's assistants shook a finger at him in mock seriousness. "You interrupted the Secretary," he chided.

"But of course," replied Jean Paul, in his best French manner. He felt sure that this tall, rather elegant, seemingly unflappable Secretary would consider enthusiasm a gift to be nurtured, not stifled. Certainly Carlhian read Dillon Ripley precisely, for the two hit it off immediately.

Some time later, Ripley asked Carlhian to come along to a congressional hearing about the project. "We left the Castle in two vans," Carlhian recalls. "The Secretary *en suite*. And he introduced me to the committee: 'Senators, I've brought my architect!' Then he unfolded a seven-foot drawing we had made at the firm, and explained to them exactly what we had in mind. It was wonderful. Dillon, with his knowledge, floored them all."

Carlhian is always quick to point out that a large part of the project is the Enid A. Haupt Garden. Before it was so named, Ripley was well aware of Mrs. Haupt's interest in the project's landscaping, and suggested to Jean Paul that she might finance a Zen garden within the quadrangle—a small, jewel-like spot for contemplation. Would Carlhian sketch one out so Ripley could include it in a letter to Mrs. Haupt?

Jean Paul was taken aback, and protested. "But you want little doodles on the borders of letters, no? I cannot do that sort of thing. It is . . ." his mind leafed quickly through his well-catalogued erudition in the history of art . . . "it is Mary Cassatt that you want!"

Ripley beamed at him. "Exactly!"

Two weeks later, Carlhian finally met Enid Haupt. She was scheduled to tour the garden site one afternoon with Ripley and others of the Institution's top echelon. The architect was included. "I had arrived early," Jean Paul remembers, "and waited in the mud with some others. This was in March, mind you, and of course the site was a morass. At precisely three o'clock, this very long, gleaming limousine pulled up beside the swamp and out stepped Enid Haupt. It was necessary that I restrain myself from taking off my jacket and spreading it before her."

Back in the Castle, Ripley asked Carlhian to explain, for the sake of the distinguished visitor, the plans for the new garden. Using a ruler as a pointer, Jean Paul indicated the various landscaping elements—the

■ *An SBRA workroom today, below; right, the same watercolor renderings that appear on the cover of this book line a corridor in the firm's office.*

parterre, the berms and pools—and where trees, shrubs, borders, hanging plants, and other beautiful things would go.

When it comes to gardens, Mrs. Haupt is yet another enthusiast. Impatiently, she seized Jean Paul's pointer and took over: "What's that tree? Where are you going to get it?" She noted the surface of a paved glade. "Is that concrete?" she demanded.

An architect with stern standards of excellence, Carlhian recoiled in shock. "Madame," he exclaimed, "the Smithsonian would never use manmade material in such a project as this garden. That surface is granite!"

Mrs. Haupt nodded in satisfaction and continued her quiz. When she finished, she turned to Secretary Ripley.

"I'm not interested in putting money into a Zen garden," she said.
Faces fell.

"I'm only interested in financing the whole thing. The entire garden. How much do you think it will cost?"

Since then it has been the Enid A. Haupt Garden. ∎

THE ARCHITECT

Jean Paul Carlhian

From the ring of its name to the record of its works, the architectural firm of Shepley, Bulfinch, Richardson and Abbott is as Yankee as the sacred cod that swings atop the Massachusetts State House (designed by the original Bulfinch). So how to explain the inclusion among its Bostonian principals of an almost unreconstructed Parisian? The answer, of course, lies in the man himself—Jean Paul Carlhian.

Legally, he became an American citizen in 1952. He says he thinks in English and dreams in English. But the minute he speaks, he displays his Gallic heart, partly because his accent manages to blend Maurice Chevalier and the Ivy League, mostly because his conversation reveals subtle traits of rationality, of confidently discriminating taste, of controlled impatience with a person, a remark, an attitude, a design that verges on the *dull*.

Oddly enough, Jean Paul looks more like a Yankee than I—who am one—can claim to do. He is tall and spare with a light complexion that quickly tans. The once blond hair lies thinly on a high forehead. Beside the blue eyes are the little fan lines you get when you spend a lot of time in the sunlight. The skin on the cheekbones is as pink as an Englishman's. The teeth are just crooked enough to lend character. Yet Jean Paul Carlhian does *not* play touch football every Sunday beside the Charles River, or skipper a forty-foot sloop during Marblehead Race Week, or ski in April at Tuckerman's Ravine, or do any of the other outdoorsy sports that characterize the blue-blooded Yankees he so resembles.

He being French, our meetings together have inevitably bracketed the lunch hour. We have lunched in splendid places with magnificent food and in modest places with splendid food. He always knows exactly where to go. During one of our early discussions, I inquired, rashly, what physical recreations could possibly keep him so trim despite midday meals that start with paté and end with crème caramel. What games had he played as a child, I asked. What sports did he now embrace?

"Sports? Games?" He looked over at me in bruised astonishment, as though I had somehow desecrated his forkful of *foie de veau*. "You have to realize," he said, "that as a boy I went to a private school where we worked from eight to noon, then from one forty-five to three forty-five, then did a supervised task—twelve lines of Latin, perhaps—from four until seven. We did this Monday through Saturday, with Thursday afternoon off.

"We studied Latin, Greek, French, physics, geography, history, and we always had one to two hours of homework. Everyone did exactly the same thing at exactly the same time. When we wrote an essay, we followed five distinct steps: introduction, an argument *for* the subject, an argument *against* the subject, discussion, and conclusion. Every subject had two sides, and we covered both of them. That was the way our young minds were trained. As for exercise, I walked to and from school twice a day, since I had lunch at home."

He resumed his meal, but I could see that memory was hard at work in him. After a sip of Beaujolais, he continued. "In history, we never learned about England or Spain or other places except when they came to a war with France. We never learned political geography. We knew how mountains were formed and we could name the rivers of French Indochina. We could tell you what borders you would cross between, perhaps, Paris and Belgrade. This would enable us to stand up straight in society and join intelligent conversations.

"The school was absolutely structured, and we were perfectly comfortable in it. It gave us the ability to organize ideas and plans and the solutions to problems. Structured thinking. Every child who entered that school

■ *Sequence of the architect's drawings shows the development of proportional relationships between the pavilions.*

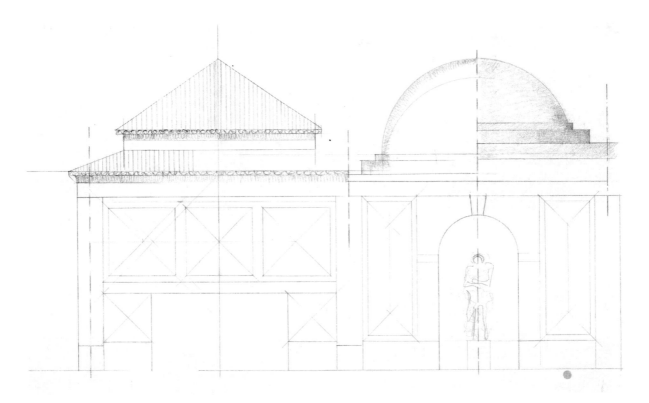

left it with the same capabilities." He produced a Gallic shrug. "I have been astounded at the lack of structure in my children's schooling. Why, they were encouraged to feel it is their birthright to discuss anything, to question anything—in any way they wish.

"French students were taught to question and criticize, but always in accordance with a recognized set of values. They would not say—as I have heard you say, just out of the blue sky—'That's a lousy portrait,' or 'What a great piece of sculpture!' 'Lousy?' 'Great?' In relation to what values? You see?"

A few more mouthfuls and another sip.

"Of course I get exercise," he said, kindly. "I walk through buildings. And incidentally, I also lift weights."

We ordered fresh raspberries for dessert. As we waited for it, the reminiscences continued.

His father and an uncle inherited the family business around 1900. Import-export, with offices in Paris and London. "But Father didn't want to sell chintzes; he wanted to design rooms. So he transformed the firm into what he called 'interior architecture.' "

André Carlhian prospered, opening a branch in New York, restoring the London branch, establishing one in Buenos Aires. He survived World War I with the colonial troops. The government used him in a scheme to nab the famed spy, Mata Hari, by staging a fashion show in Madrid. They hauled Carlhian Père away from the front to design the room where

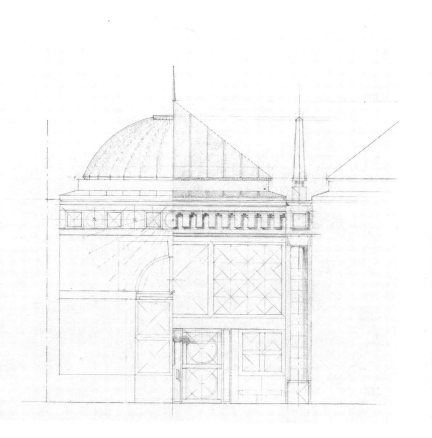
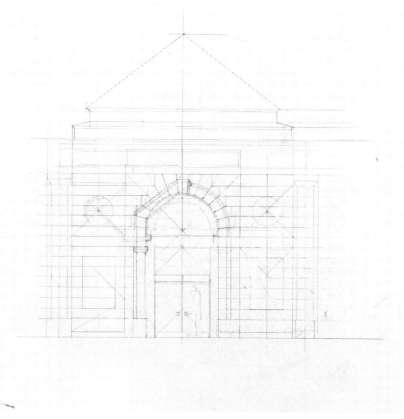

the show would take place. The room was elegant. As far as Jean Paul knows, it did provide a backdrop for setting her up.

Jean Paul had two considerably older brothers and a considerably younger sister. Isolated by age, he was largely brought up by an English nanny. "Father never considered children as children," he said. "He never gave me ice cream or a toy. At the dinner table, where he ran the conversation, he would talk to us as adults—about Italian art, for example." Father was not an ungenerous man, however. Jean Paul remembers that as he grew older any book or perhaps print that he admired in a shop would often be given to him.

Certainly as a toddler Jean Paul was spoiled—at least after the fashion of the day. "I was put into little piqué dresses and patent leather shoes. Miss Conway curled my hair. Mother? Mother was very beautiful and *très grande*—and not interested in children until they were fifteen. She left them to Miss Conway and spent her time spoiling Father. Father had definite ideas of the way life should be conducted, and Mother saw to it that he got his way."

One of Father's compulsions was an extended motoring tour every summer. They had a large touring car, adapted to hold eighteen pieces of luggage, all specially designed to fit in it. Jean Paul recalls that his father always said he hated bringing along so much luggage, yet insisted on wearing a clean shirt every day.

The summer when he was thirteen, Jean Paul was given the choice of going to the seaside with Miss Conway or joining his parents on a motor tour and becoming a "courier" for them. He enlisted for the tour. "Believe me, the training I received looking after Mother and Father was rigid enough to prepare me for any traveling I have ever done in my life!

"When it came to hotels, Mother demanded luxury. Father would accept her choice, but only if their room had a perfect view of the lake, or the mountain, or whatever. If he wasn't given that, he wouldn't stay. Since they were marvelous customers, the various concierges saw to it that they got what they wanted. From 1921 until the war they spent two weeks every summer in room number 7 at the Grand Hotel in Venice.

■ *Sketches illustrating evolution of African Pavilion design.*

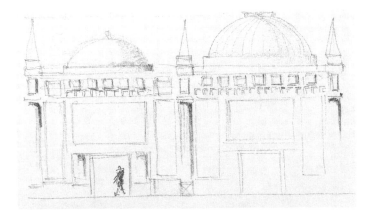
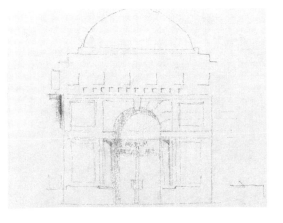
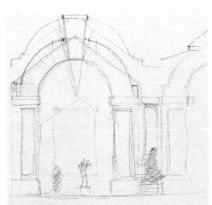

Once I suggested that they should take a cruise. I went to all the agents, gathered all the cruise descriptions and accommodation plans, and Father studied them carefully and agreed to go on a certain ship, 'but only if I have cabin A-21.' Mother went to the agent and passed along Father's preference. The agent smiled understandingly and said he was sorry, but A-21 was reserved. Mother said, 'Very well. Forget the whole thing.' I don't know how the agent worked it, but they got cabin A-21.

"So. Each summer I had to make reservations, get us through Customs, pack the car, unpack it when we arrived, tip the bell boys, and keep a log of the trip. When we arrived at a hotel, I would unload bags and oversee the porters while Mother made sure that the room would be acceptable to Father—the right floor, the right view, the right number of windows. And by the time I had seen to the car, they would have gone off to the suite without remembering to tell me what number it was.

"Father had a terror of Customs. He never tried to smuggle anything past the inspectors, but he couldn't stand all those questions. So he'd simply walk across the border with his passport and a cigar, and he'd sit on a bench and smoke and wait for us to get those eighteen bags through. It created a peculiar situation—he in one country and we in another."

Father seems to have been as structured as that French school, but he had a wonderful knack for success. Visiting the States in 1929, he came home feeling uneasy about the stock market and instructed his broker to sell every share he owned. Two weeks later came the Crash. One had to take seriously the whims of such a man, and his sons did so when he planned their careers. Jean Paul was selected to become an architect. "Fortunately," he says, "I enjoyed it."

The raspberries had come and gone by now, and so had the coffee. The mood of remembrance, however, was irresistible, and I mentally altered my own plans for the afternoon (I, too, attended a pretty structured school) in order to keep my companion going with those formal, finely constructed sentences with which educated Europeans put Americans to shame.

"In 1937, I applied to an 'Atelier' of the Ecole des Beaux Arts and

"The quadrangle project has been a grand opportunity, a great challenge, and an ominous responsibility. It has provided the chance of calling upon one's experience and lasting convictions: that architecture is at its greatest when meeting constraints, that creativity is at its richest when inspired by precedent, that quality is at its best when expressed in true materials honestly assembled." J.P.C.

 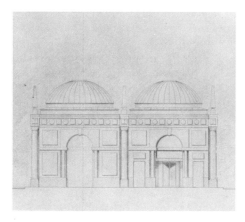 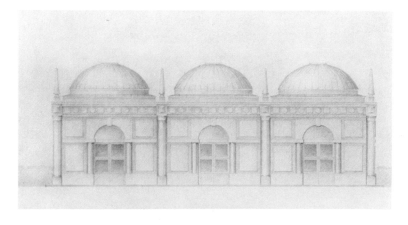

passed the entrance requirements. Educated? I'd had seven years of Latin and three of Greek, and I was a good student. But of course the Munich crisis arrived in 1938, and soon I was in the French army, assigned to an electrical engineering unit. I, of course, knew nothing about electrical engineering. When the Nazis overran France in 1940, our captain, an old World War I veteran, somehow spirited forty trucks away from a neighboring artillery unit and so led his 350 men to the Spanish border. We stole fuel on the way. We brought along five rifles and twenty-five rounds of ammunition, and of course we included all the demonstration panels explaining electrical engineering."

The war stories took the rest of the afternoon, and deserve a book of their own. Suffice it here that the sternly rigid elder Carlhian was outraged by the even more sternly rigid Nazis and determined to foil the German occupation at every turn. "He had named his four children 'Marie'— Marie Robert, Marie Michel, Marie Brigitte—to fool 'le fisc,' the French internal revenue people. Of course the names thoroughly confused the Germans, too."

Under their bewildered noses, Marie Jean Paul managed to jump the Swiss border three times, only to be sent back by the Swiss. He was able to escape Vichy France and reenter occupied Paris without anyone laying a glove on him. He borrowed a friend's identification card and, under the name Pierre Dupré, attended the Ecole des Beaux Arts.

"I lived in an apartment and never went out. If you went to a movie the Germans would suddenly charge in, turn on the lights, and seize all the men for their labor camps. So I simply stayed out of sight until Paris was freed. But I was a good student. And with no demands on me except to keep hidden, I accumulated enough honors to clear the first hurdle of the prestigious Grand Prix de Rome competition. In 1945 I applied for a visa to the United States. I believe I was the second French student to get one. I wrote to Harvard to see if I could study city planning, and

■ *Earliest concepts for the Sackler Pavilion indicate polychromatic treatment and Moorish influence.*

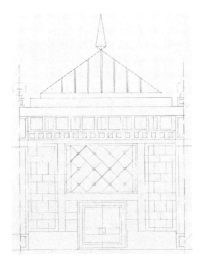

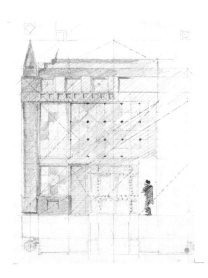

Harvard gave me a scholarship. I intended to stay only for that one year—1945–46."

Carlhian says that after a year at Harvard he was sufficiently Americanized to understand *New Yorker* cartoons. He bought a Buick, and when, in June of 1946, his mother and father came over to visit him, he took them on a tour across the United States. "Father disapproved of American bureaucracy and deplored the American labor unions," he recalls. "I had become a different person in America. I had taken courses in economics and political science that were unheard of in France. I now found it hard to understand my own parents."

Harvard offered him a much-sought scholarship, the Wheelwright, and Jean Paul decided to stay in the States one more year. He earned a Master's. Then in June 1947, at the instigation of his father, he sailed for France. Back in Paris, he continued his pursuit of the Grand Prix de Rome, but failed to clear the second hurdle. He completed his thesis for the Ecole des Beaux Arts, a study of American housing, and in June 1948, it was judged the best one of the year. A month later, Harvard offered him a teaching position. He decided to emigrate.

"I didn't feel comfortable in France. I argued with old friends about the class system, about the horrors of all that structured society. I tried to talk to Father. He was in his library, the walls lined with ten thousand volumes, and he was quite impossible. *'Tu veux devenir petit professeur de dessin dans une ecole de province?'* he snorted. I tried to point out that by joining the Harvard faculty I would hardly become a 'little drafting instructor in a provincial school'; that, in fact, Harvard's endowment was as large as the entire French national budget. I finally said that I had to go to America, that I simply was going. . . .

"And he cut me off. Suddenly I had no more pleasant allowance from the family business. I sold my record player and all my records. I went to the Institute of Internal Education to try to get passage money to the

"Real architecture should be made to last, to survive the ravages of time and outlive the vagaries of fashion." J.P.C.

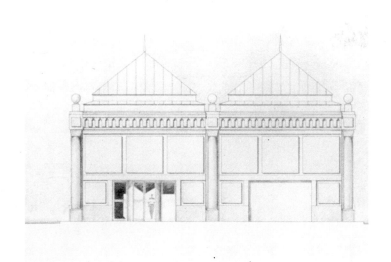

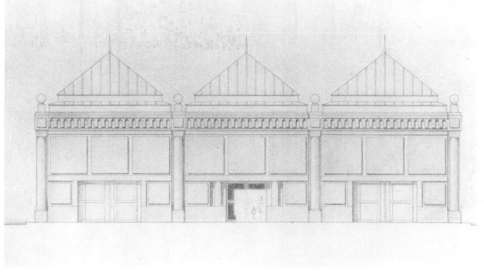

States. They laughed. 'The Carlhians do not need passage money,' they said. 'But yes, this one does,' I said. 'I don't have a sou, and I do have a job waiting for me.' I was given a ticket, and in August 1948, I sailed for the United States. I brought everything—all my clothes, twelve crates of books. And so, that fall, I started teaching in the Harvard School of Design under Walter Gropius."

Carlhian rose in the faculty hierarchy. He became an assistant to Gropius in the latter's famous "Masters' class." By then he was married to a landscape architect who was also working at Harvard. Betty gave birth to two children. "When the first one, our daughter Penelope, was born, Father did not respond to the news. When the second one, our son Jerome, arrived, Father wrote me a long letter. It was very important, he said, that we bring up the Carlhian heir properly."

Jean Paul and Betty decided to visit Paris with their children. They had a fine time. The elder Carlhians provided them with a car for a tour through part of Europe, and found Miss Conway an assistant to look after the children. But the émigré was not forgiven. "Mind you," he says, "Father was a wonderful person, interested in absolutely everything, intelligent enough to understand every kind of person and situation, inspiring to his children. He endowed me with wonderfully valuable things—his interests, his excitement about life itself. But he had blind spots, and my emigration to the United States—the country that he loved and admired so deeply—was one of them. Strange. . . .

"Father died in 1968, just a few months after Mother died. He did not want to live without her. He was eighty-five. She was eighty when she died. It was the first time I ever knew her age. You know, Father's grandmother was a Cézanne. Did I tell you that? No? Ah, well. . . ."

Jean Paul loved his years on the faculty of the Harvard School of Design. But he remembers a little wryly the exhibit of his highly judged Ecole thesis. The design was of a family compound, not unlike that of the Kennedys in Hyannisport. The French had thought it odd and American, not just because of its location on the Hudson River, but because it was mostly wood and consisted of standard prefabricated parts. But the French awarding jury, under the renowned Auguste Perret, gave it top marks. Not so the Americans. . . .

"I succumbed to suggestions by students and faculty that I show this work, and put it up in Robinson Hall. It was a great mistake. Harvard, you see, was so sure of itself, so reluctant to accept another viewpoint. So the reviews of my thesis were terrible. People scorned and ridiculed it. Yet today former students from those days often speak to me about it."

Carlhian's connection with Shepley, Bulfinch, Richardson and Abbott began with a visit he made to an exhibit of World War II battleground monuments. One monument was by Henry Richardson Shepley, who happened to be on the visiting committee of the School of Design. Jean Paul sought him out to discuss it. As a Frenchman who had waited four years to be liberated by the Americans and who understood their sacrifices, he had strong ideas about such a memorial.

Shepley listened thoughtfully and invited Carlhian to write up a critique. Carlhian did so. He was made a consultant to the firm, then a part-time designer. In 1955 he realized that his teaching schedule precluded him from being given full responsibility for architectural assignments. Reluctantly, he resigned from Harvard.

"Because I was an academic and knew Harvard, the firm, particularly Harry Shepley, pushed me toward university buildings and complexes. Harvard was expanding, seeking new spaces and structures. I designed the first Harvard house to break the skyline—Quincy House, intended to blend with the surrounding Georgian structures. It won the Parker Medal Award. Then I did Leverett House, which went up even higher—eleven stories. And after that, the Harvard Corporation specifically asked for me as designer of Mather House. And then the same request came from across the Charles River at the Harvard Business School. There I did the McCollum Center and Baker House."

After nine years with the firm, Carlhian was made a principal. He has come a long way from France—a lot more than three thousand miles. In the United States he is one of the relatively few architects to have studied at the Ecole des Beaux Arts, and perhaps the only one who is French and has the perspective of a European. He knew Gropius well. He is in demand as a teacher at Harvard and Yale. He is sought all over the country as a speaker.

"In the 1970s," he told me, "the National Endowment for the Arts gave me a design fellowship. It consisted of a ten-thousand-dollar grant for which I was supposed to think. Just take time off from what I was doing and think. I'd never heard of such a thing."

He thought, all right. He thought about a book dealing with the influence of the teaching of the Ecole des Beaux Arts upon American architects in the half-century between 1886 and 1936. He nurtured that seed, and with a second NEA grant, he completed a mental outline. He's working on the book now.

Now a long-time American citizen, Jean Paul finds himself, somewhat to his surprise, a devoted patriot, fiercely proud of American successes and bitterly defensive about American blunders. The country means a great deal to him, and he epitomizes his feelings with another memory, this time of driving through the desert lands of Utah and stopping for a beer at a little roadside bar.

"A local man, my age, started talking to me, and mentioned that I have an accent. I told him I was French. He said he'd been there during the war. And I suddenly pictured this man leaving his home out here in Utah and going all the way to France to fight for me. I wondered if when I was a young man I would have gone even as far as Spain to fight for the Spanish. Frenchmen seldom do that. I think it's extraordinary that Americans take it so for granted.

"How could one not like such a country?" ∎

■ *Jean Paul Carlhian, left; above, the desk of a busy architect.*

PROBLEMS

A plan to build a new major museum complex on Washington's sacred Mall caused almost as much stir in the nation's capital as did the capture of the city by the British in 1814. When the Smithsonian first revealed the quadrangle project, Washington authorities were skeptical, at best.

Watchdog organizations rushed to the defense of the status quo. Official review bodies—the Commission of Fine Arts, the National Capital Planning Commission, the Joint Committee on Landmarks (now the D.C. Preservation Review Board), and the National Advisory Council on Historic Preservation joined forces with several private groups—the Victorian Society in America, the Committee of One Hundred on the Federal City, the Sierra Club, and one called Don't Tear It Down. Their task was to meet another invasion of Washington space, this time by the Smithsonian's visionary Secretary, S. Dillon Ripley, and his resourceful architectural team, headed by Jean Paul Carlhian.

Was the proposed structure really needed?

Ripley, a veteran of such questions, had already taken on Congress to make that point. But as soon as first plans for the garden and the underground complex appeared, the various agencies fired dozens of other questions at Carlhian and his team.

Would the huge structure in any way overwhelm the Mall?

Had this been the 1930s, the sanctity of the Mall would probably not have arisen as an important issue. This ribbon of greenery, stretching from the Lincoln Memorial to the Capitol, encompassing the Washington Monument, was then considered a sort of promenade for members of Congress, a convenient site for temporary government office buildings ("tempos"), and an alternate route for traffic when Independence and Constitution avenues were choked with blatting, fuming Packards, Essexes, Studebakers, and Rios.

But in the 1970s the Mall came upon better days. Traffic and tempos were banished. And since so much of the greensward serves as a broad front lawn for the Smithsonian (six Smithsonian museums and the Castle face out upon it, not to mention the two buildings of the National

Some key members of the quadrangle's architectural team engage in decision-making. From left, Richard Potter, Albert Huang, Ron Finiw, Robert Holloran.

Gallery), Secretary Ripley set about making the National Mall into a people's park.

Ripley asked for—and got—a carousel with bobbing steeds and tinkly music. He inaugurated the Smithsonian's annual Festival of American Folklife, celebrating songs, dances, story-telling, cooking—cultural traditions from all over the world. All year long, visitors to Washington from every state, every nation, now stroll along the Mall, and gaze and rest and fly kites and scale Frisbees. Clearly, nothing must threaten such a place.

Nothing would. The quadrangle site faces Independence Avenue, and is parallel to but not directly on the Mall. Though the aboveground buildings of the new museum complex would be partly visible to someone who walked past the Castle craning for a glimpse, they would scarcely be noticed by the casual sightseer on the Mall.

Would the new development destroy the Smithsonian's recently built but already cherished Victorian Garden?

It certainly would during the years of construction. Before work could start, every bit of the Victorian Garden, along with the paved section that had been a most convenient staff parking lot, would have to be torn up and forgotten for the near future.

We on the staff, of course, lost our assigned parking spaces—to Washington commuters perhaps more valuable than oil wells. But that tragedy paled beside the loss of "our" matchless garden. Bright with flowers, soft underfoot, this was the idyllic glade through which we walked to our offices every morning. Tree-shaded, serene, this was the bower we visited for moments during the day to sit and soothe frazzled nerves and listen to the mockingbird (whose name was Henry—after Secretary Joseph Henry).

We watched, numbly, as this gentle place was ripped apart, its plants uprooted, its surface deeply rutted by huge trucks. "It's only temporary," we told ourselves. But in my case, that hardly dimmed the horror with which I stared from my window as a brutally powerful mobile crane seized a wonderful old tree and tore it out of the ground. Nothing was sacred. Nothing.

■ *J. Carter Brown, seated at head of table, directs a Fine Arts Commission review of a proposal for the quadrangle project. S. Dillon Ripley stands at right. Opposite, a pre-groundbreaking view of the site shows mock-up of the Renwick Gates.*

Well, one thing was. When I was first employed at the Smithsonian, early in Mr. Ripley's tenure, my assigned parking space was under a giant European linden tree that stood in the northeast corner of the quadrangle and had cast its shade there for a hundred years. I would turn briskly into the lot, wind over to the tree and, with what I considered an expert's touch, slither to a stop with my front bumper an inch and a half from the trunk.

On my fourth morning at the job, my editor, Edward K. Thompson, received a memo from Mr. Ripley: "If your new man, Park, touches the linden tree, he's finished." The same caveat held true when the quadrangle project got under way. Mr. Ripley made it clear that no matter what the architectural or engineering needs, the linden tree must not be touched.

How to avoid it? "The idea of encasing it in a cylinder occurred to Junzo Yoshimura," says Jean Paul Carlhian, "but the cost would have been between six and seven hundred thousand dollars. So we simply put a notch for the tree in the plan. We took a corner out of the rectangle."

And so, all through the months of construction, Smithsonian people have noted the old linden standing tall above the muddy turmoil, a hurricane fence around it, and a sprinkler system hooked up to keep the dust from fouling the leaves.

The design of the new garden was half of Carlhian's assignment. But the input from the regulatory agencies, the Smithsonian, and a Washington citizenry almost fanatically determined to restore its favorite glades and dells and flower beds endlessly guided him. His client, the Smithsonian, wanted distinct themes—African and Asian—expressed in the eastern and western sections of the garden to correspond to the collections that lay below them.

Junzo Yoshimura's original plan showed two sunken courtyards in the garden; one on each side of the central parterre. These would allow light to reach down to the second level of the museums. The National Capital Planning Commission and the Commission of Fine Arts agreed that these would be destructive to the garden and should be eliminated.

"I must say, I was glad of that decision," Carlhian says. "The idea of ethnic food being served in those hot courtyards while African dances raised clouds of dust created a horror in my mind."

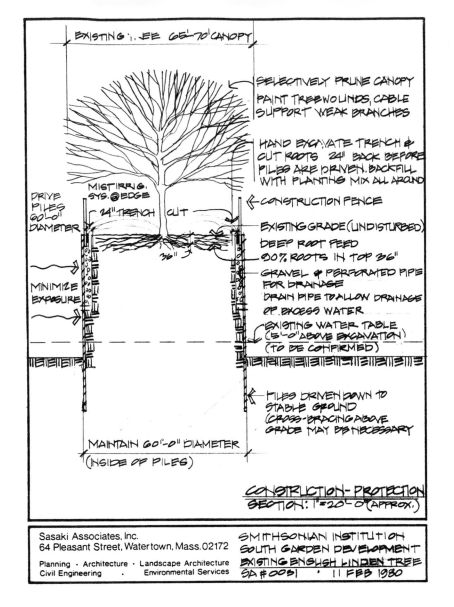

EXISTING TREE 65'-70' CANOPY

SELECTIVELY PRUNE CANOPY

PAINT TREE WOUNDS, CABLE SUPPORT WEAK BRANCHES

HAND EXCAVATE TRENCH & CUT ROOTS 24" BACK BEFORE PILES ARE DRIVEN. BACKFILL WITH PLANTING MIX ALL AROUND

MIST IRRIG. SYS. @ EDGE

DRIVE PILES 60'-0" DIAMETER

24" TRENCH CUT

CONSTRUCTION FENCE

EXISTING GRADE (UNDISTURBED)

DEEP ROOT FEED

90% ROOTS IN TOP 36"

36"

GRAVEL & PERFORATED PIPE FOR DRAINAGE

DRAIN PIPE TO ALLOW DRAINAGE OF EXCESS WATER

EXISTING WATER TABLE (5'-0" ABOVE EXCAVATION) (TO BE CONFIRMED)

MINIMIZE EXPOSURE

PILES DRIVEN DOWN TO STABLE GROUND (CROSS-BRACING ABOVE GRADE MAY BE NECESSARY

MAINTAIN 60'-0" DIAMETER (INSIDE OF PILES)

CONSTRUCTION-PROTECTION
SECTION: 1"=20'-0" (APPROX.)

Sasaki Associates, Inc.
64 Pleasant Street, Watertown, Mass. 02172

Planning · Architecture · Landscape Architecture
Civil Engineering · Environmental Services

SMITHSONIAN INSTITUTION
SOUTH GARDEN DEVELOPMENT
EXISTING ENGLISH LINDEN TREE
SA #0051 · 11 FEB 1980

A number of different approaches for the garden were conceived.

First: a walled garden north of each pavilion. This idea didn't get anywhere. Gardens plus walls would occupy too much space and would make the gardens inaccessible. Please give us a "unified and open treatment," said the National Capital Planning Commission.

Second: an oriental garden on the western side and an "English garden" occupying the rest of the space. This, too, bogged down, but led to . . .

Third: a number of ideas for the treatment of the oriental garden. What about a small "lake"? "But," said one of the Smithsonian administrators, "in winter it will have to be drained, or it will freeze and crack and cause leaks. And it will gather many scraps of discarded Kleenex, and be a nuisance." No lake. Similarly, a garden unit of raked gravel and a meandering section were proposed. Critics argued

Landscape architect's preliminary plan to protect the European linden, above. Left, the linden today; opposite, fence protects the tree during construction.

that raked gravel would be hot and dusty and the meandering bit didn't make sense. Rejected. Another idea was a moss garden, abandoned because Washington summers are too hot for moss to survive without constant watering.

Fourth: a turn toward the Moors for the African (east) side of the garden. Why not something in the style of the Alhambra? Why not?

Fifth: a Zen garden, a sublimely beautiful and totally secluded spot on the western side that people could see from the eastern galleries of the Freer, but which no one could enter. A Japanese designer was approached for this scheme, but the impenetrability of the place seemed a waste of space to the regulatory agencies. No Zen garden.

There were other trials and rejections, but the final plan carried out

■ Precedents: *In the drawings on these pages, Jean Paul Carlhian shows derivative forms for the gardens adjoining both pavilions. The moongate garden to the north of the Sackler Gallery utilizes the notion in traditional Chinese art of framing startling and mysterious views in doorways or windows. The circle-in-a-square form for the pool is taken from the Temple of Heaven in Beijing (above, left) where important features occupy a median north-south axis.*

■ Precedents: *The fountain garden adjoining the African Pavilion is seen as a summer retreat, shaded by several densely planted hawthorns. The design is inspired by the Alhambra gardens in Grenada and features bubbling fountains and canals of running water. The north end of the garden is terminated by a vertical fountain of carved granite as an allusion to the chadar of India. A full description of the garden begins on page 116.*

African and Asian motifs in the garden. Carlhian deliberately switched them, however, placing a square rotated 45 degrees to become an Asian diamond on the eastern, or African, side and an African circle, within a square, on the western, Asian side. This served to tie the whole scheme together, to give it unity.

To bring light down into the building, so that people wouldn't undergo the natural stifling effect of being far down in the innards of the earth, the architectural team had to make room for skylights in the garden, yet keep them concealed from casual view. These skylights required treated glass to bar harmful rays, and the plans hid them behind berms and within shrubbery. Three such schemes were rejected by the agencies before the final arrangement of skylights was approved.

The law required eight exit stairways, which the architect designed to emerge in small sheltering structures. Two of them were located right in front of the Castle's south facade. Though the plans called for them to be faced with old sandstone from a demolished Washington prison, thus closely matching the Castle walls, the Commission of Fine Arts considered them too "boxy." J. Carter Brown, Director of the National Gallery, took Carlhian aside. "What do you always see in a cathedral close in England?"

Jean Paul considered for a moment. "Tombs," he said.

"That's what we need," J. Carter Brown said. "Tombs."

And so Carlhian redrew the two exits to look like the tombs that line Rome's Appian Way. He gave them sloping roofs and ornaments or acroteria, on the two gables of each roof. Instantly the structures were dubbed Romeo and Juliet. Scores of questions were raised about conditions down below Romeo and Juliet, below the garden, in the museum complex.

How would the proper temperature for multimillion-dollar exhibits be maintained? What about humidity?

Going underground made both of those requirements relatively easy to fulfill. Temperature and humidity remain quite stable below ground and can be kept within the narrow range that museums require. Nevertheless the machinery needed for climate control in a building of this size was enough to fill the entire Independence Avenue edge of it on the lowest level.

Junzo Yoshimura had originally planned a parking garage on the third level. It would have provided room for 350 cars, but also would have taken up the entire floor. Its access ramp, entering the building from Independence Avenue, was originally placed near the Arts and Industries Building. But the agencies felt the ramp might damage this 1881 structure since it has no basement or deep foundation, so the architects moved the ramp to the western end of the garden, near the Freer.

The planned garage ate up so much valuable space that it soon was eliminated altogether. This saved money and allowed room for much-needed staff offices.

How about leaks?

Obviously, this problem was one of the first attacked. The excavation for the project would go sixty feet deep, and would be large enough to hold three Lincoln Memorials. Since the big hole penetrated twenty-four feet below the Washington water table, the structure would "float" in it, the floors and walls completely impervious to water. On its roof would go layers of waterproofing materials, including fiberglass, before the garden soil was piled over everything. Skylights would be permanently fixed, their caulking forever maintained. A submarine should be as watertight!

How do new acquisitions get into the museums? Would there be appropriate access for large trucks?

They would use the auto ramp that remained in the plan when underground parking was eliminated. At the suggestion of the National Capital Planning Commission, Carlhian gave it a lateral bend so that people on the Independence Avenue sidewalk wouldn't actually see trucks roll down to the end of the ramp and unload. He further concealed it by roofing it part way down with a trellis on which wisteria would grow.

"The world's most elegant truck ramp!" he said with some relish. "They will leave the street and disappear from sight in a bower of blossoms."

Yoshimura's concept of an aboveground structure—an iceberg's tip through which people would descend to the buried treasures—struck the Carlhian team as certainly the right approach. But the representative of one agency felt that the "Japanese tea house" style was a little "too World's Fairish" for the Smithsonian. Carlhian says he welcomed the chance to build upon the idea, but make it into something "serenely classic."

The National Capital Planning Commission felt that pavilions, placed in the garden "like settees on an oriental rug," were needed, but that style would be unimportant, since the "container need not reflect the contents." A lady from the Committee of One Hundred, devoted to the garden, said that the Smithsonian didn't need any sort of building that would take up room from the plants. "Just have a glass-walled entrance," she said, "with an elevator and some stairs and a guard."

Carlhian looked at her quizzically. "Madame," he answered, "you have just described the entrance to a subway. This is not the Washington Metro. It is one of the great museums of the world."

The architect wanted people to be able to absorb the beauty of the new garden, "and then get underground without the feeling that they are diving into a bunker."

"You don't go *down* to Heaven," he once pointed out to me. "You ascend. One habitually climbs *up* to good things—to light and virtue, to meet the president, to attend the opera. One goes *down* to darkness and evil, to the dungeon, the crypt, and the bargain basement after cheap underwear. Here, we had to alter that concept. Our job was to lure people *down* to a matchless treasure trove."

Each pavilion would serve as a splendidly appropriate entrance to the exhibition area below—one Asian, one African. Each would make a discreet statement to signify what awaited those who entered. The pavilions would not be designed as galleries with display space on their walls. Instead, as Dillion Ripley said, these would be "grand vestibules," providing a chance for visitors to prepare themselves for their museum venture.

Of course, as every old Smithsonian hand well knew, the Institution routinely runs out of space as the decades pass. The dim future might require a rethinking concerning the pavilion use.

Carlhian designed his pavilions, however, with only the museum-goer in mind. To me he once pictured a mother with two children setting out to visit the museums' treasures: "Her taxi has had a frustrating struggle with traffic; she has undertipped the driver, and he drives away seething; both her children suddenly need to go to the bathroom."

Diving into a bunker would hardly get her started right. But entering

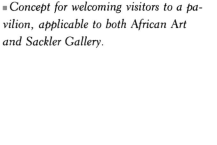

■ *Concept for welcoming visitors to a pavilion, applicable to both African Art and Sackler Gallery.*

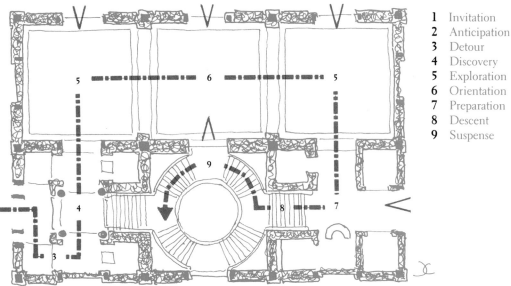

1 Invitation
2 Anticipation
3 Detour
4 Discovery
5 Exploration
6 Orientation
7 Preparation
8 Descent
9 Suspense

■ *The pavilions under construction.*
Right, the Arthur M. Sackler Gallery;
below, interior and exterior views of the
National Museum of African Art.

a pavilion gives her both the space and the time that she needs. "Here," said Carlhian, "she would be able to draw breath, kick off her galoshes, and check her coat. Restrooms below would welcome the needy children. She'd be able to shift mental gears away from her irate taxi driver and back to her anticipation of a new experience."

Designed as a hint of things to come, each pavilion would establish a mood of excitement. By the time the harassed visitor reached the stairs, going *down* would seem altogether proper. It would, in fact, prove irresistible.

"There's a great disadvantage to climbing a staircase," Carlhian says. "When you look up at others, ascending ahead of you, all you can see are their bottoms. But when you enter one of our pavilions, you see people at the turn of the grand staircase, descending. And you see their *faces*, all presumably alight with excitement."

Would the pavilions render the Forrestal Building a less oppressive presence when seen from the garden?

The Forrestal Building is an enormous government edifice across Independence Avenue from the Castle, built in bleak "governmentese." It looms opposite the quadrangle site, pretty much destroying the vista south to L'Enfant Plaza. It is generally in the shade, ominously dark.

One of the earliest design requirements for the new Smithsonian complex was to take the curse off this gloomy, monotonous bulk. Certainly the two pavilions in the garden would absorb any attention that strayed from the plantings and glades. With the help of trees planted along Independence Avenue, the Forrestal would mercifully be ignored.

Would the pavilions block the view of the Castle?

Looking toward the garden from Independence Avenue, the pavilions would frame and enhance the view of the Castle, not block it. Yet critics insisted that the pavilions would be too tall, that they would compete visually with the Castle, that they took up too much garden space.

Their height, said Carlhian, was dictated by the structures surrounding them. Moreover, once the garden was built, with its grassy berms sloping up to the pavilion walls, the structures would seem much smaller. During the years of construction, the site of the garden was so thoroughly erased

■ *Below, eastern facade of the Freer Gallery; western facade of the Arts and Industries Building, opposite.*

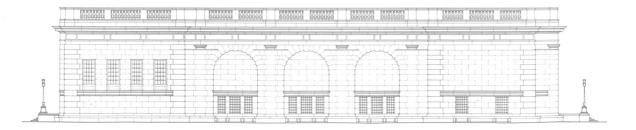

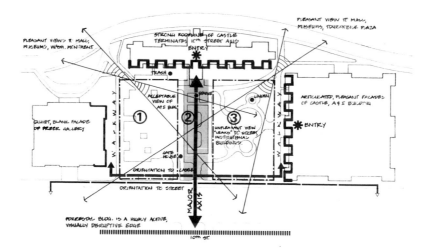

■ *Study of visual conditions of the site, from an early environmental impact statement.*

that it was hard to picture it. Jean Paul had to persuade viewers that soil would lie deep around the walls, that trees would flower and flourish around them, and that the pavilions would seem modest in such surroundings.

Would the underground building weaken neighboring historic landmarks?

The subsoil problem was never out of the thoughts of the architectural team. Digging that deep seemed certain to produce tremors that would endanger the old walls of the Castle and the Arts and Industries Building. Yet this area proved to be the best available site for such excavation. Prehistoric migrations of the Potomac River were presumably responsible for the firm gravel bank that had allowed construction of the Castle and the A and I Building here in the first place. Because earlier nineteenth-century buildings used fill as a support for foundations, they had to be on a firm surface such as that in this part of the Mall. In addition, the quadrangle was free of underground transportation and water routes.

The architects knew of the techniques they would have to employ. As the final plans were approved and contractors began to bid, everyone involved realized the delicacy, physical, social, and political, that would be required to get this job done.

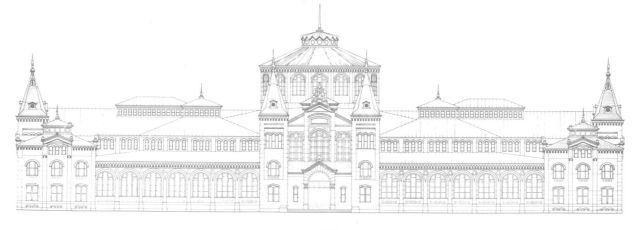

Arthur M. Sackler Gallery

The broad sweep of Asia, from its Mediterranean shores to the Pacific and from neolithic times to the present, is the realm of the Arthur M. Sackler Gallery, the Smithsonian's newest museum. The gallery was founded in honor of a gift of approximately one thousand masterworks of Asian art made in 1982 by the late Dr. Sackler, a New York research physician, publisher, and art connoisseur.

Dr. Sackler, whose collecting interests ranged from pre-Columbian ceramics to European bronzes and Impressionist painting, in addition to Asian art, began collecting in the 1940s, following his graduation from medical school. He was widely known for his generosity to scientific and cultural endeavors at many of the world's great institutions.

Dr. Sackler's outstanding gift to the nation came at a time when the Smithsonian Institution was seeking to expand its long-standing commitment to scholarly study and exhibition concerning a region that is home to more than half the human race. The history of art in Asia and the Near East may be the world's longest, but the fascinating and ultimately rewarding images produced by their diverse cultures remain unfamiliar to many Westerners.

Changes in the world political and economic climate, not to mention a burgeoning tourist caravan to Asia, have piqued the public interest in this vast continent. Seminal discoveries by archaeologists, as well as broader contact among scholars in the international museum community, have expanded the possibilities for offering Western museum visitors a

rich banquet of loan exhibitions of paintings, sculptures, textiles, metalware, and ceramics from many periods and cultures.

The Smithsonian has set a high standard for Asian art scholarship since the opening of its Freer Gallery of Art in 1923. Due to certain requirements in the will of museum founder Charles Lang Freer, however, only objects from the permanent collection have been exhibited at the Freer, and none of the art has traveled to other museums. Mr. Freer felt strongly that all of the museum's holdings should be readily accessible to scholars at all times. He had good reason for his wishes then, but his request has placed limitations on the Smithsonian's Asian art exhibition program at a time of unprecedented opportunity.

With his gift of art and funds, Dr. Sackler has helped to provide for the Smithsonian's first museum offering space for important loan exhibitions of Asian and Near Eastern art in a collection-related context. His gift, which forms the basis of a growing permanent collection, presents a multitude of images, from the delicate to the powerful, and these offer the visitor insights into the multifaceted cultural, political, religious, linguistic, and social histories of a variety of Asian artistic traditions.

The Sackler Gallery offers limitless potential for engaging the public in the process of learning about the many aspects of Asian culture through its exhibitions and its programs of education, publications, and research.

■ *Left to right, ritual wine container, bronze, China, Western Zhou dynasty, 11th–10th century B.C.; roundel with a vine scroll, silver and gilt, Iran, 6th–7th century; Adam and Eve Riding upon a Dragon and a Peacock, "Falnama" manuscript, opaque watercolor on paper, Iran, Tabriz, mid-16th century; hound, jade, China, Tang dynasty, 7th–8th century.*

Teams of creative humans often seem to work in a world of tension. Spectacular and important magazines are born of the cross-purposes of editors, writers, art directors, and advertisers, often bitterly argued. Memorable television programs result from a director's determination to wrench perfection out of lighting, sound, cameras, special effects, and talent, even at two in the morning. And what Academy Award–winning film was ever produced without a couple of star-spangled tantrums?

A team of architects, too, works under tension. I dropped in at Shepley, Bulfinch, Richardson and Abbott one day in early winter to check out this theory. My friend Jean Paul Carlhian was finished with the quadrangle project except for its many last-minute readjustments, and was involved in a project far removed from it. He and a team of very bright younger architects were designing the corporate headquarters of an international company, a complex that would fit comfortably in a hilly, wooded section of the New England countryside.

I started watching the architectural process without any particular interest in the purpose of it. But seeing the team at work, listening to their carefully considered opinions, noting their moments of silent thought, their obvious care to state their convictions with pure honesty, sensing their ever-present stress, I found myself ensnared by the task. This plan was poles away from our new museum complex, but I soon became familiar with it, and the innate problems of such a novel commercial design fascinated me.

The Shepley, Bulfinch, Richardson and Abbott team had taken over a conference room beside the entrance foyer of their Broad Street office. On the big table was the model of the corporate headquarters, meticulously fashioned from light cardboard and correctly painted. The miniature buildings were grouped around a sort of campus ("another quadrangle!" I thought) on an uneven hillside—obviously in the laudable attempt to blend modern high-tech manufacturing with wild nature. Among the trees and nestled in the folds of the hill were a large administration building with impressive staff meeting rooms, a library, an office building, terraces, gardens, retaining walls, underground parking. . . . Every build-

■ *W. Mason Smith III, in his SBRA office.*

ing was perfectly scaled, its proportions easily adjudged and quickly comparable to others in the group.

That godlike perspective—which, of course, is the purpose of an architectural model—allowed Carlhian, this morning, to focus on the design of the library, a semidetached feature of the building complex. "I think this element must be widened," he was saying as I entered the room. "The pitch of this roof is not the same . . . you see? We can't have pitches that are not the same."

This was obviously an unarguable point to SBRA staff members. One of them searched in a flat drawer, produced a plan of the facade in question, and pinned it on the wall. Everyone stared at it and then at an accompanying plan of another facade. The roof angles in question were not quite the same. A member of the team tapped one of them. "The shape of this scheme is a cross," he said. "Both of the models are based on your sketch."

They returned to the overall model spread out on the table. "Both schemes are exactly the same size," said Carlhian. "Why does this element of this scheme look so big?"

"I think," said one team member, "it's because the knuckle on this other wing steps down."

"I think," said another, "that we can cut four feet off the eave line and still maintain the proper overall square footage. It'll have a cathedral ceiling then, with a downward slope in the corners."

Obviously this was a point worth contemplating because everyone did so, staring silently at the model. Finally Carlhian bent over it, and with the assurance of Zeus regarding the Parthenon, picked up the two little cardboard buildings under scrutiny.

"This is so big," he said, hefting one, "and it makes this one . . ." he hefted the other, "look so small. I'm not very happy with it. Are you?"

Aha! I thought. The old professorial ploy: present an opinion and give an A to the students who agree with it. But the members of this team were not students. They were competent professionals, and their integrity was as essential to the job as their taste. The replies pretty well covered the spectrum. Two people maintained that they were perfectly happy with it, at least as a form (whatever that meant). A third agreed with Carlhian. A fourth, the one who had suggested cutting down the dimensions, returned to that point.

"I'd like to see what would happen if we just dropped four feet off the eave line," he said.

Carlhian thoughtfully replaced one of the cardboard buildings and displayed the other in the palm of his hand. "This is a nice building, but I think it shouldn't go there." He set it down across the campus. That inspired another long, deliberative silence.

"It does give a sort of acknowledgment of the building across the way," said a team member.

■ Jean Paul Carlhian, left; opposite, SBRA members at work. Below, project team members discussing preliminary quadrangle models. From left, Richard Potter, Albert Huang, Ron Finiw, Robert Holloran.

■ *Richard Potter, principal in charge of the Smithsonian project, in his office.*

"Yes," agreed Carlhian. "Without being identical. Without having the same roof pitch."

"It looks so *small*," said another team member, doubtfully.

"Yes! Isn't it pleasant!" said another.

"I like the big one just because it's big," said another.

"But there are so many ridgepoles," protested Jean Paul. "You must admit that this thing, compared to that thing, is really *very* big."

The one who had been suggesting that the too-large building could be cut down in size without a redesign tried again: "We can make it six feet narrower, and still keep this cruciform, and the plan still works. The other way would be to chop four feet off the bottom, and make it shorter, and again the plan still works."

Another long pause. Carlhian finally nodded, "All right. Try it. Then I'd like to take out these two things," indicating the two transepts of the cruciform.

"You can't take them out and still keep the volume you need," someone protested.

"Why not? Then we lengthen the building. No?"

"Go to just a single ridgepole? Oh well. . . . All right."

"So! If we have a ridge running like *that*, then this must not be a square any more." Carlhian was on a warm scent. All of Boston could have burned around his knees, and he wouldn't have noticed. He seized the by-now somewhat wobbly model of the building in question.

"We push *that* thing in *here* . . . like that, and *that* thing in *there* . . . like that, and we still have the same basic scheme. And then we have *that* . . . right? And *this* . . . yes? And so I think that this space must not be a square. . . ."

Three of the others murmured "Right!" They were caught up with him, now. He was hot, and he was teaching by doing, and they were grabbing at it. And so the problem was solved, and I could feel the pressure ease off.

Then Jean Paul suggested extending a certain roof all alone, without extending the supporting walls.

"You mean like a porch?" someone asked.

"Yes."

"With nothing supporting it? Like a big arch?"

"No. It's already a pediment."

"Oh, sure. I think it'll work. What'll people do with this porch?"

"Maybe we should put a rocking chair on it," suggested Carlhian. "Do we really need a rationale? Let's just do it."

"You know . . . we could put doors under that roof."

"That's an idea," said Carlhian. "Then we have an excuse. The doors have to open under a porch in case it rains."

They all looked at me, dubiously, remembering that I was an outsider and had just overheard a secret of architecture—finding a rationale for a design instead of vice versa. I pretended to be studying part of the plan.

Carlhian didn't always run the whole show. He readily accepted decisions from the others when they were sensible. I almost wrote "when they were right," but architecture is notoriously gray when it comes to right or wrong. Carlhian's own concepts suffered frequent rebuffs. For example, the client had complained that the stairway from terrace to garden was too monumental. The idea of a corporate headquarters having a terrace and a garden so intrigued me that I missed part of the conversation. They were discussing the grand foyer from which the garden stairs descended when I noticed Jean Paul looking quizzically at one of his young colleagues. "What are you laughing at?" he demanded.

"I disagree with you," said the young person, with a grin.

"You do?" Jean Paul seemed shocked. "With the whole thing?"

"No, no. Not the whole thing. With this idea of columns in this foyer."

"You want to take these columns out? But that leaves a great empty maw like the ballroom of a Hyatt hotel. This is only a house. . . ."

"It's a house with very big rooms. Why not make this a straight corridor? The scale of this is so close to the scale of that. . . . You see? So, I'd drop that and just have a link, a straight corridor."

Jean Paul puzzled over that for a while, shuffling through the plans. Then he straightened up. "All right," he said. And again the tension dropped.

■ *Jean Paul Carlhian and Robert Holloran review quadrangle project drawings, left; Ralph T. Jackson, member of project team, opposite.*

"That was a good session for you to watch," Jean Paul told me at lunch. "The project is big, and different—like the quadrangle—and as you could see, a good many sparks fly in getting it right. These are very bright people, and they are often specialists—experts in various aspects of design—stairs, lighting, roofing, that sort of thing. Talk to the team that worked with me on the Smithsonian complex. They all had a great deal to do with it."

I did talk to them. I started with Richard M. Potter, who, as he says, "puts the legal and financial stamp" on new projects. "I catch the flak and pay the bills," he explained. "I work up the contracts and the schedules and assume the legal responsibilities."

Robert T. Holloran, project architect for the quadrangle, told me that he has a lot of experience designing hospitals, and that the strict demands of the Smithsonian reminded him of a hospital job. "The structure has many of the same requirements," he said. "And the circulation of people is quite a bit similar."

Holloran pointed out that an architect must play the role of the user. "I've often tried to feel what a doctor must do in a hospital." Similarly, when he was given a school to design, he went back to visit his own school in the old Massachusetts fishing port of Gloucester.

"I made the teachers draw exactly what they wanted," he said. "Curiously, they all drew pretty much the existing classrooms, so I used these as a core, and expanded from them."

Ron Finiw—it's a Ukranian name, he told me, spelled the Polish way, and pronounced "Finyou"—was one of the first on the project. Working very closely with Carlhian, he was given responsibility for the Kiosk, the stairs, and the auditorium. He said the Kiosk, with its round plan and spiral stairway, "was one of the most complicated buildings I've ever worked on."

"It was supposed to be a garden structure and so it couldn't be very big," he continued. "Its window patterns had to fit with the diamond and circle motifs in the pavilions, yet be different. The stairway down to the first level had to remain open, because it allows you to experience almost the whole building at a glance. At the same time, of course, we had to allow that shaft of light to reach down."

Although Dick Potter is SBRA's "money-man," figuring estimated costs and constantly supervising them, all architects, Finiw added, must be aware of costs at all times and develop strategies to stay within limits. "A progress estimate circulates, telling you how you're doing," he said. "So you must fine-tune your ideas as you go along. Sometimes you scrimp a little here to splurge a little there. At the Smithsonian you couldn't scrimp on waterproofing, but we might have splurged by excavating a few feet deeper."

Lawrence Man, in charge of the overall plan, but specifically of the Concourse on the third level, told me this was his first underground architectural job. "I visited a museum in Oakland, California, that has

an underground gallery, and I studied the way it had been designed. I tried to put myself in the place of people going down into the ground, reorienting themselves. How would I find my way around in a dark area? Could I feel comfortable? How would I like working where I couldn't see out of a window? That was why we needed that high, airy environment of the Concourse."

"The Smithsonian job is so big that it has to be a team effort," he said. He was intrigued by the strict security requirements: "Study the systems. Find the best one. Then hide it." He said that the team members often brainstormed and argued, pairs going out to dinner together and discussing the job far into the night. "Albert Huang, who was responsible for the pavilions, and Ron Finiw were always interacting," he said.

The result of all this funneled creativity was 489 architectural drawings—plans, elevations, details, other renderings. One drawing after another dealt with aspects of the project. How would a Zen garden go within the Haupt Garden? A plan shows how. How would the same area look without it? Another plan.

Looking through that enormous file of drawings and accurate plans, one could trace the thinking concerning the project from Yoshimura to the opening of the completed tour de force. "When did you begin work on it?" I asked Jean Paul.

He glanced at a file, then opened a drawer and checked the date on a plan. "January 30, 1980," he answered. "That was apparently my first team meeting." He put the rendering away with an admiring shake of his

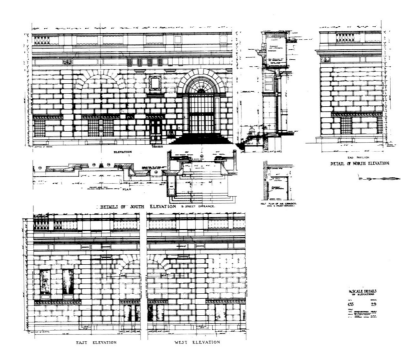

head. "Apparently *someone* does something right around here," he said.

Seeing the volume of completed work in this office cabinet, I asked Jean Paul if he worked at home, in the evenings.

"Not very much," he said. "A sketch or two sometimes. I read quite a bit. You'll see."

I did see. The Carlhians live in Concord, some twenty miles northwest of Boston. It should be an easy commute, but those who do it generally agree that hell hath few furies like Massachusetts Route 2. This, the grandly named Concord Turnpike, has sickened into a badly clogged artery, confounded by stoplights and further befouled in the winter by snow and sleet. Steely-eyed state troopers lurk at every less-cluttered stretch of highway that might tempt the heavy-footed. So the pace of traffic is about as discreet as that of a Proper Bostonian's electric car, and Jean Paul, a facile and generally impatient driver, has learned to keep more or less close to it.

Jean Paul and Betty own a newish, largish, highly livable colonial-style exurban home right on the Sudbury River, which, as Henry David Thoreau pointed out, is really a branch of his beloved Concord River. "It is worth the while to make a voyage up this stream," says Thoreau, and goes on to tell of "ducks by the hundred, all uneasy in the surf, in the raw wind, just ready to rise . . ." and "all around the alders, and birches, and oaks, and maples full of glee and sap, holding in their buds until the waters subside."

The river wasn't in spring flood when I saw it, so I can't speak for the

■ *Albert Huang at his desk, opposite; arches of Freer Gallery exterior elevation, left, are echoed in drawings of African Pavilion interiors, right.*

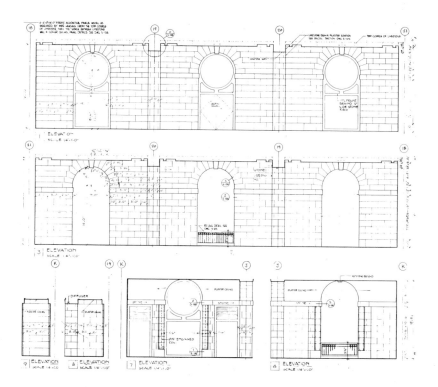

ducks or the sap-laden maples. This was December, and looking from a picture window in the early nightfall, I puzzled over what seemed almost like a country road—streaks of light and dark beyond the sloping lawn. It was, of course, the river—a brush of early snow lingering on new black ice.

"Do you go canoeing on it in the springtime?" I asked Jean Paul.

"Of course," he answered, without elaboration.

He led me into the work room where Junzo Yoshimura had felt so at home. It *was* a mess. But it had a certain antic organization. I envied Jean Paul's huge work table. I was awed by his portfolio-size books of architectural designs, too huge for any reasonable shelf. I was charmed by the bronzes—graceful objects and figurines—that he collects.

"I know what every pile is," he said, indicating the stacked papers on the floor. "But when people come in to clean, they put one pile on top of another, and then it becomes confusing. Now I have new filing cabinets, you see? And so I suppose I shall have to put some of these in alphabetical order and things like that."

It was cold in the room, and Jean Paul explained that he keeps the heat low unless he's working. "We may expand into an adjoining room," he said, "if Betty will stand for it. She should, because she keeps her beehive equipment here in the winter." That accounted for the faint, rather pleasing smell of beeswax.

Betty Carlhian remains a notable landscape architect in her own right, and, being involved with gardens, became appreciative of and interested in bees. Many of the books that line the sprawling, comfortable living room deal with her fields of interest. We sat on a deep sofa that faces a broad and cheerful colonial fireplace. At dinner, Jean Paul produced a dusty bottle of a wine that Americans only faintly hear of, and we talked until we yawned.

Early to bed meant early to rise. It was still almost dark when we set out to attack that miserable drive. And it was in low, early sunlight that we pulled into a parking garage about three blocks from the Broad Street office.

The commute is bad enough to keep the Carlhians from venturing into Boston for entertainment, except in extraordinary situations. I asked if they see movies. "About four times a year, in Concord." Do they have cable TV? No, but they get Boston's famous WGBH, where "Masterpiece Theatre" originated in the East. The Carlhians are fans of the above, enjoy most BBC comedies, hate Monty Python.

Generally, work keeps them both busy. And that indicates that the work is fascinating and life is good. When you measure the magnitude of the quadrangle project's problems, and the ingenuity and sometimes genuine grandeur of their various solutions, you begin to sense the obsessive involvement, the near intoxication that the architect feels when committed to such a task. ■

■ *Two of the almost 150 staff members of SBRA, left; the model shop, above.*

SOLUTIONS

In the children's classic *The Wind in the Willows*, the Mole and the Water Rat, lost in the Wild Wood on a snowy night, are given haven by Badger in his underground home. Rat is uneasy about being so far below the world he knows, but Mole expresses his delight to Badger:

" 'Once well underground,' he said, 'you know exactly where you are. Nothing can happen to you, and nothing can get at you. You're entirely your own master, and you don't have to consult anybody or mind what they say. Things go on all the same overhead, and you let 'em, and don't bother about 'em. When you want to, up you go, and there the things are, waiting for you.'

"The Badger simply beamed on him. 'That's exactly what I say,' he replied. 'There's no security, or peace and tranquillity, except underground.' "

Unfortunately, people are more like the Water Rat than the Mole and Badger. Jean Paul Carlhian and his architectural team recognized from the start of the quadrangle project that human acceptance of an underground environment was the toughest problem they faced. People inevitably feel constraint below ground. Some feel it quite deeply. Yet in crowded cities, space for large public buildings is vastly expensive. Architects generally find their needed space by building *up*.

In some cases, however, a tall building isn't the answer. In Paris, the Louvre expanded underground because the existing building is a treasured landmark and it and the area all around it would be severely damaged by a tall building. In Colonial Williamsburg, the rules of the Foundation bar new buildings in the restored area. When the DeWitt Wallace Decorative Arts Gallery, an extraordinary showplace for furniture and art that doesn't fall within the colonial period, was being planned, this regulation was kept in mind. The best site was on the land that surrounds the old Insane Asylum—a historic building, but not part of the colonial area.

"It's so close to the restricted area," said a Williamsburg resident, "that any new building on that lot would have been as disturbing to the colonial feeling as a set of Golden Arches."

■ *Natural light descends three stories from the garden to reach the Concourse. A fountain, windowed walls, and walkways effect a street scene.*

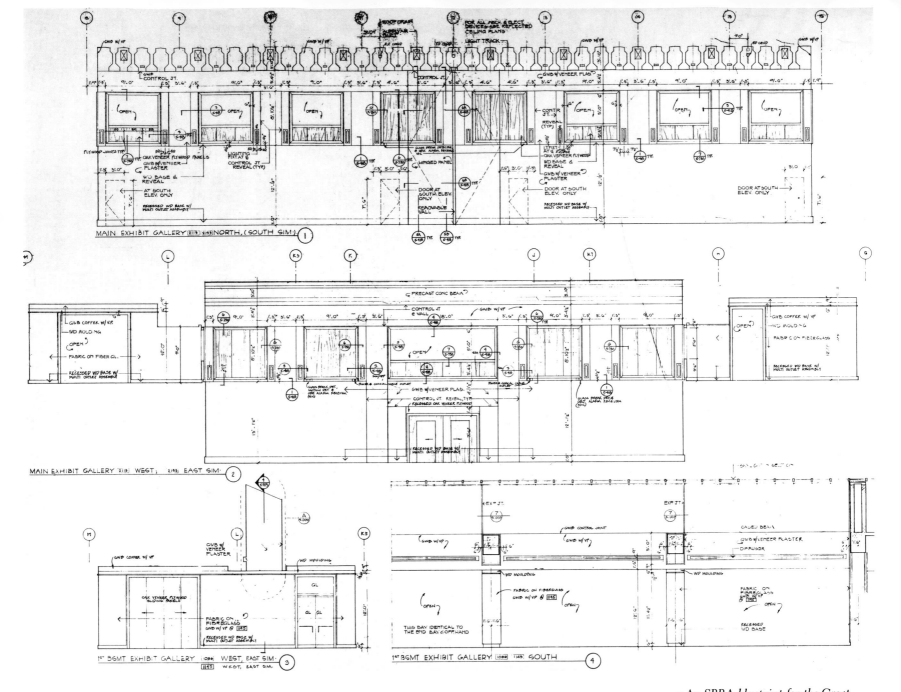

MAIN EXHIBIT GALLERY ⟨2113⟩ ⟨2153⟩ NORTH, (SOUTH SIM.) 1

MAIN EXHIBIT GALLERY ⟨2113⟩ WEST; ⟨2153⟩ EAST SIM. 2

1ST BSMT EXHIBIT GALLERY ⟨1060⟩ WEST, EAST SIM. 3

1ST BSMT EXHIBIT GALLERY ⟨1060⟩ ⟨1145⟩ SOUTH 4

■ *An SBRA blueprint for the Great Hall, above, features balcony and window overlooks. Left and opposite, construction in progress.*

The architectural solution: build an authentic wall around what had been the Asylum garden, let it conceal part of the new gallery, then set the rest underground. The visitor eases from ground level to the floor below without realizing it. A splendid stairway heading back up provides a sort of psychological security blanket to the wary. It brings plenty of light down with it, and it's hardly ever out of sight.

But the requirements at the Smithsonian were far stricter: enlarge and improve the garden; save the linden tree; don't mess in any way with the existing buildings. Going underground here meant a complete commitment to Mother Earth, three levels deep—far enough down to feel very isolated from the world above.

The architectural answer to our (and to the Water Rat's) unease at such depth is to provide enough open space to remove the sense of physical pressure, of confinement. Jean Paul Carlhian planned open areas where people could sense ample space around and above them, and so lose that squeezed feeling.

Although the structure contains two completely separate museums, the African and the Sackler, from the architectural point of view the first and second levels of the building are a unit distinct from the third level, the S. Dillon Ripley Center, which houses Smithsonian bureau offices, classrooms, lecture areas, and office and exhibition space for the International Center. For these two units Carlhian designed two vast open areas, intended to dominate the visitors' underground experience.

In the third level, the Concourse, as Carlhian had dubbed it, serves as a broad, airy street, flanked by attractive urban doorways. Plants and flowers grow along it; a fountain plays in it. Its ceiling is so high—three stories up to the skylights that are cleverly concealed in the garden—that you might as well be on a downtown Manhattan street, where skyscrapers form a deep canyon, or perhaps more properly, in a picturesque London mews on a foggy day.

Similarly, a huge "great hall" would be the centerpiece of the first and second levels, the spaces allocated to the Arthur M. Sackler Gallery and the National Museum of African Art. Carlhian designed a vast open

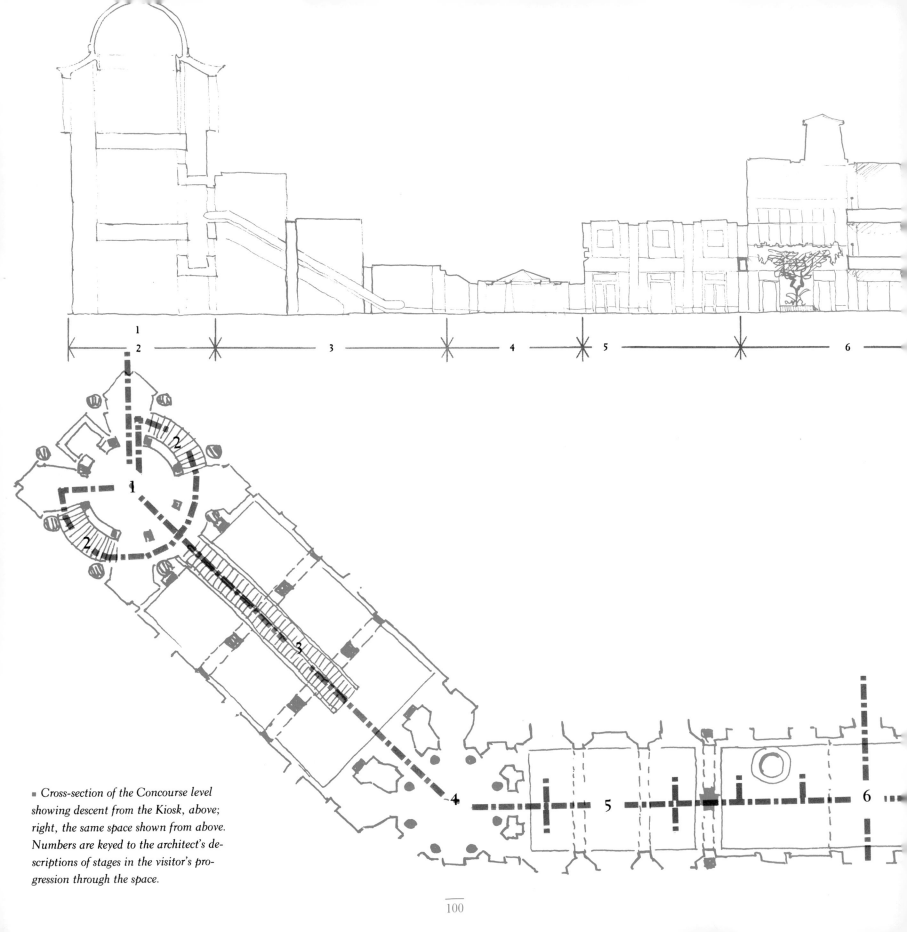

■ Cross-section of the Concourse level showing descent from the Kiosk, above; right, the same space shown from above. Numbers are keyed to the architect's descriptions of stages in the visitor's progression through the space.

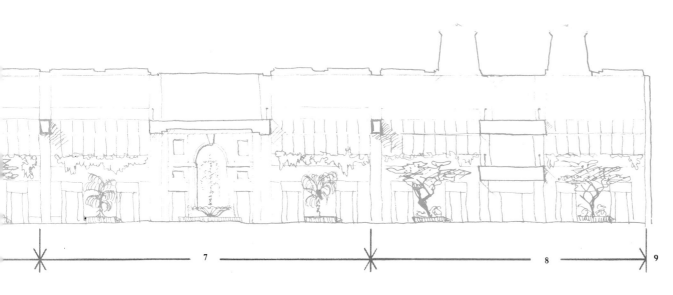

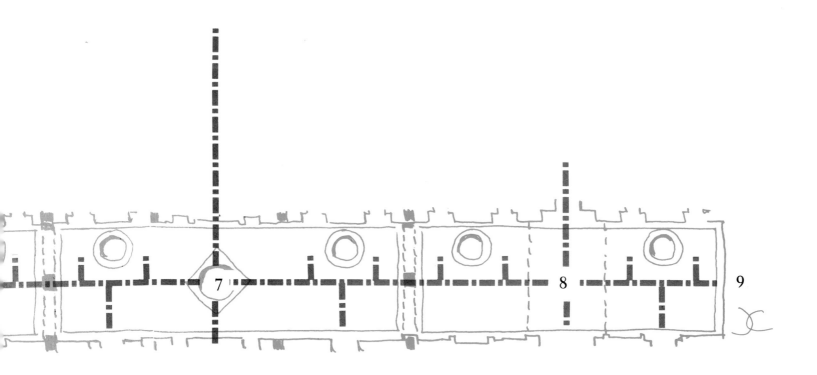

room, 116 feet long, 78 feet wide, two stories high, to be entered on the second or lower level. He wanted his visitor to experience a sense of openness provided by nearly ten thousand feet of breathing space.

But . . . here the architect's vision and the curators' needs proved in the long run to be irreconcilable, as is explained in this book's Afterword. The Great Hall was split in half, each museum handling its space differently.

In the National Museum of African Art, huge windows, almost true balconies, open onto the exhibition area. "This," Carlhian explained to me, "would allow people who are not used to going down into the ground to quickly have the chance to look out on familiar open space, and to see other people across the way also looking out, and so to reestablish the sense of being among fellow humans and not among . . . among . . .

"Moles?" I suggested.

"Exactly. Not among moles."

On the lowest level, the area under the Great Hall provides a gallery for the International Center. Long, narrow, its ceiling supported by eight columns, the room seems ideally suited as a banquet hall if the occasion arises (and at the Smithsonian Institution it often does). Besides this huge room, the Ripley Center contains the Concourse, and RAP, SNAP, and SITES (the Resident Associate Program, the National Associate Program, and the Smithsonian Institution Traveling Exhibition Service). Other public spaces on this level include the Education Center: classrooms, a photo lab, a balconied auditorium, and large symposia rooms.

Smithsonian Resident Associates and the general public descending to this level for classes, workshops, or lectures share the staff entrance. This is a small, copper-domed structure in the northwest corner of the quadrangle, between the Castle and the Freer. "Since this was to be a public entrance," Jean Paul explained to me, "we wanted it to be an elegant building. But it had to be small—small enough to blend with the garden around it." It was quickly dubbed the Kiosk.

The Kiosk is round, forty-two feet in diameter, and its copper dome rises thirty-eight feet above ground level. Glass windows surround the bright limestone cylinder that forms the core of the building. A circular stairway descends around that core, so people going down are, as Carlhian puts it, "drenched with natural daylight."

At the first level the stairway ends. People step onto a forty-four-foot escalator, and descend in a straight line, right past the second level, on down to the third. They pass through a hall where displays can be placed to entertain and delight them as they move past.

The escalator reaches the third level at an angle, so people must be reoriented to the grid of the rooms and corridors. They step out of it into that deliberately dark and almost ominous rotunda where the architect has toyed a little with human sensibilities. For when people leave the rotunda—which they do in about six steps—they burst out of its confines and into the Concourse, a street that ribbons away before them for almost

■ *The Concourse under construction.*

the length of a football field, that spreads twenty-eight feet wide, that seems to have no ceiling.

The Concourse is the great design feature of the third level. When Carlhian first led me down to it, I found, even though I knew what to expect, that its impact made me breathe deeply, that all my senses seemed to record the wash of empty space around me. "That," said Carlhian, "is what it's supposed to do."

Bridges cross the Concourse. A fountain splashes precisely halfway along its length, almost directly under the Castle's tallest tower, the Flag Tower. Constantly changing displays of green plants and colorful flowers grow in six planters designed to also serve as seats. Greenery cascades from the balconies of the matching directors' offices, overlooking the "street scene." The plants and the fountain were all planned to give the feeling of being outdoors to those who work and study in the offices and classrooms that flank the Concourse.

And then, at the eastern end of the street, the Richard Haas mural reminds you where you are—sixty feet underground. Deep enough, surely, to win the approbation of the Mole and the Badger. Yet with enough breathing space to suit the Water Rat.

About 96 percent of the building had to be designed to go underground. What in the world was left for passers-by to look at? The answer, of course, is the two pavilions. Here was a chance to express, above ground, the notion that something wonderful lay below ground. Junzo Yoshimura had already designed two—one to be 120 by 60 feet, the other 10 feet shorter—and Carlhian's job was to refine what the Japanese had done.

"When Yoshimura first planned pavilions, he gave quite a Japanese feeling to one, and tried to use the conical shape of African huts for the African one. People didn't like them very much, so when we took over we tried other things."

Shepley, Bulfinch, Richardson and Abbott first tried, on the African side, a two-story pavilion with a single dome, and on the Asian side, stepped pyramidal roofs. The review committees thought the structures much too big.

"We studied the problem," Carlhian recalled, "and realized that trying to keep an ethnic approach to the look of the pavilions wasn't going to work."

Carlhian said that David Childs, chairman of the National Capital Planning Commission, solved the problem by pointing out that the late Renaissance style of the Freer has nothing whatever to do with the Asian art and the James McNeill Whistler works (including the famed Peacock Room) that it was built to house. "In other words, the container of treasures need not necessarily reveal the nature of its contents."

This philosophy opened the door to new approaches. Carlhian went back to the notion that the pavilions should somehow reflect and reconcile the varying architectural styles around the quadrangle: the late Renaissance Freer, completed in 1921, opened in 1923; James Renwick's Romanesque Revival Castle, finished in 1855; and the Arts and Industries Building with its wonderfully Victorian adaptation of the Romanesque, which opened in time for President Garfield's inauguration in 1881.

The three buildings leave an impression of sharp angles and round arches. The Castle with its steep-roofed, sometimes tapering towers seems to come straight from a "Grimm's Fairy-Tales" illustration. Yet its tall windows are strictly rounded-arched. The Arts and Industries Building also unites angled rooflines and round arches. And the beautiful Freer Gallery is a composition of discreet round arches, either in windows and entrances or simply etched on the blank walls. Carlhian decided to repeat the sharply angled look in six small pyramids atop the Sackler Pavilion. He echoed the rounded look in the African Pavilion.

But exactly where to place them? As an old Beaux Arts student, Carlhian is always aware of an axis, if one exists. No more so than on the quadrangle. Here a distinct axis runs north and south, a vista from L'Enfant Plaza through the elegant sandstone gates to the Enid A. Haupt Garden and on to the South Door of the Castle, a splendid entryway opposite the usual Mall entrance.

This view would have to be maintained, so the pavilions would stand on each side of it. Jean Paul then found key points on the facades of the Freer and the Arts and Industries Building. This allowed him to place the two pavilions along a pleasing east-west line.

Jean Paul led me, one afternoon, to a point on Independence Avenue directly in line with the center of the garden gates. Beyond them rose the Castle, its great central South Door directly in line. The two pavilions, almost completed, rose to my right and left, their facades neatly framing the whole sweep of the Castle. Behind me stretched L'Enfant Plaza, and I couldn't help but realize how pleased the Gallic ghost of Major Charles L'Enfant must be to see his love of vistas so splendidly repeated by a fellow countryman. On the right, the African Pavilion partially blocked the most distant part of the Arts and Industries Building, just as the Sackler Pavilion got in the way of the northeast corner of the Freer. Yet there was a harmony about the new structures that made them far less intrusive than I had expected.

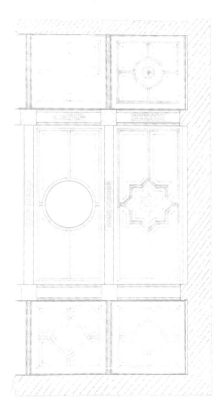

■ *Discovered in the Smithsonian Archives, this unused drawing for a ceiling in the Castle by Adolph Cluss, circa 1888, was never seen by either Yoshimura or SBRA. The circle and square motifs come to life a century later.*

■ *The Kiosk's scalloped roofline and window treatment echo the curvilinear turrets of the Castle.*

Both pavilions reflect the Castle's facade, which they frame. African Art echoes the round arches of the Freer, the Sackler picks up the angled roof of the Arts and Industries Building. So the eye is led from east to west, from each new building to the old structure that is farthest away from it. This trick neatly ties the whole architectural sprawl of the site together in a single meaningful composition. The new structures are thus in tune with the old. It's a pretty tricky ploy—and it works.

The pavilions are ninety by sixty feet, considerably smaller than Yoshimura's. They rise twenty-four feet to their cornices, which is not as tall as the cornice line of either the Freer or the Arts and Industries Building. Their distinctive roofs, one with six domes, the other with six pyramids, add another dozen feet or so to their height. This allows them to block a good bit of the overpowering view of the Forrestal Building that has been afflicting everyone who looked out of one of the Castle's south windows. At the same time, neither pavilion is high enough to interfere with the splendor of its neighbors.

Having established the motifs for the pavilion roofs, Carlhian and his crew simply let them call the tune for each building—circular for the African, diagonal for the Sackler. The windows follow these shapes. So does the stonework of the blind windows. So do the patterns of ceilings and floors.

■ *The pavilions' rooflines and facades, and their entrances shown in insets reflect the repetition of diamond and circular motifs. Below, the Sackler Pavilion; opposite, the African Pavilion.*

Skylights suffuse the pavilion stairways with natural light. Sackler Pavilion, right; African Pavilion, opposite.

The stairways are Carlhian's pride and joy—and little wonder. Each adheres to the motif of the pavilion from which it descends: a circular stairway for the round-domed African Pavilion, a diamond-shaped descent for the Sackler with its pyramidal roof. In each case, the stairs go down around a central shaft of light. It drops from a skylight atop the pavilion in one of the six domes or pyramids. And sixty feet underground, the light is reflected back up—and so reinforced—by a pool at the bottom of each stairwell, a round pool in the east, and you guessed it in the west. People on the stairs can always look down and see light from the sky bouncing back up at them.

The two pavilions were designed to be "color coded." Thus the reflecting

pool at the bottom of the stairwell in the Sackler Pavilion is jade green tile; that in the African Pavilion is blue. Similarly, the ceilings of the structures would continue the jade and blue motif, and the windows on the sides of the two stairwells would be stained glass, pale blue in the African Pavilion and amber in the Sackler. Changes in this scheme are explained in the Afterword to this book.

And so the pavilions evolved, from large museum structures which probably would have contained galleries as well as the usual cloakrooms, restrooms, and guard rooms, to what Mr. Ripley called "grand vestibules," entryways only—but designed with considerable elegance. Badger's house, remember, had only a door between the roots of a tree. ■

Africa's visual traditions and cultures are addressed at this remarkable museum on a scale and with an intensity new to the study of African art in this country. Permanent installations include the finest acquisitions from the museum's collection of more than six thousand objects, representing the major regions south of the Sahara. Temporary exhibitions are organized by the museum's own curatorial staff or as cooperative ventures with other institutions. In addition to the visible exhibition areas, the spacious building also houses an art conservation laboratory, library, photographic archives, educational facilities, a photography studio, a design department, collection storage areas, and administrative offices.

The staff of the National Museum of African Art seeks to increase the body of knowledge about the visual arts of Africa and to convey a wider understanding of them. Through scholarly research, the museum is uncovering new facets of the African artistic heritage. Via symposia, conferences, and lectures, national and international scholars assemble to discuss their work and ideas. Workshops, tours, films, performances, and publications bring the arts and cultural traditions of Africa to life for an ever-widening audience.

"The art of Africa represents one of mankind's most harmonious fusions of visual imagery with social purpose and spiritual beliefs," says Director Sylvia Williams. "The works demonstrate artistic perfection and technical achievement that are tributes to the creative genius of their makers."

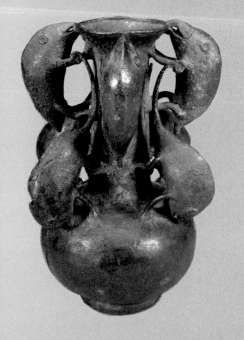

■ *Left to right, female figure with children, wood, Yoruba, Nigeria, height, 15¼ inches; Cameroon grave figure, wood, glass beads, cowries, dated 1908, height 62 inches; vessel with chameleons, cast brass, Lower Niger Bronze Industry, circa 1668–1773, height 9 inches; woman and child figure, wood, Kongo (Yombe), Zaire, wood, late 19th or early 20th century, height 10¼ inches.*

L A N D S C A P E
The Enid A. Haupt Garden

The quadrangle project confronted Jean Paul Carlhian with the task of designing a museum complex and a garden together. The first would have to be built around (and under) the second. This seemed a daunting assignment perhaps, but he dove into it at once, first researching how the quadrangle, or "South Yard" as it was called, had appeared in the early days of the Smithsonian.

When James Renwick, Jr., designed the Castle in the 1840s, he planned its main entrance on the Mall side, and kept its southern facade free of a carriage driveway. Carlhian speculated that the Castle architect foresaw the southern slope of the lawn becoming a sun-drenched garden, all the way to the banks of the Potomac (which was a good deal closer—and marshier—in those days). "In other words," Carlhian says, "Renwick might have envisioned what we in France would call a 'facade sur jardin.'"

Thanks to the growth of Washington, that wonderful concept went out the window. Railroad tracks wound along the Potomac's bank, and on muddy B Street, S.W., now Independence Avenue, people clopped past the Castle on horseback or in carriages. The view of the river was pretty much destroyed, except from the towers of the Castle. Atop the highest, Secretary Joseph Henry studied meteorology and solar effects, and here, at least on one occasion, President Abraham Lincoln came to visit him and to watch signallers of the Union Army practice their semaphoring.

The garden idea was forgotten. For a while, a few bison grazed in the South Yard, indicating to new generations that this most American of all animals was being systematically wiped out in the western territories. Various outbuildings sprouted in the area south of the Castle. Here was the workshop where Secretary Samuel P. Langley built his "aerodrome," an *unmanned* flying machine that made the first successful sustained flight of a heavier-than-air, powered vehicle in history. During Langley's tenure the South Yard had a deliberately low profile: he ordered the buildings to be left unpainted and the grass unmowed—to deter reporters!

Another building—a carriage house—served Secretary Charles Abbot as a laboratory. It later became the famous Smithsonian "bug house," where skeletal specimens were attacked and thoroughly cleaned by tiny

■ *The simplicity of Asian artforms characterizes the garden adjoining the pavilion of the Arthur M. Sackler Gallery.*

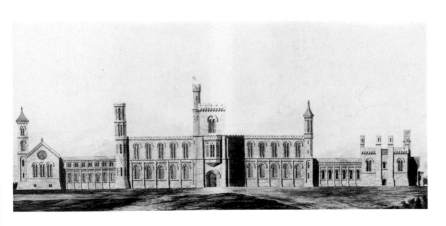

beetles. In another of these buildings scientists began studying the effects of radiation biology. This makeshift lab finally moved out of town to continue experiments as the Radiation Biology Laboratory.

In 1917 the U.S. Army built a simple hut on the South Yard in which to repair the engines of demonstration allied fighter airplanes. At war's end the army gave the building to the Smithsonian, and it was the first home of the collection that would later become the National Air and Space Museum. Huge rockets, first installed in 1959, and too big to fit inside the building, towered on the South Yard like sentinels. The collection also spilled into the Arts and Industries Building, where the Wright and Lindbergh airplanes hung from the ceiling.

Parking in the South Yard was made available to more and more staff members until cars seemed to fill every cranny of the area. They bordered all the outbuildings, they nuzzled against the great trees, they took over a couple of acres of land, served by a gate which opened onto Independence Avenue.

Then as the Bicentennial of 1976 approached, the old area underwent a drastic change. The beautiful new National Air and Space Museum began rising along Independence Avenue, between 4th and 7th streets. This meant that the ugly old hut would go and Arts and Industries would be free for other exhibits.

All of the miscellaneous outbuildings were abruptly torn down in December 1975, and I recall wondering what was done with the little beetles in the bug house. All I know is, a new, more efficient, pristinely clean bug house appeared in one of the courts over at the Museum of Natural History, and its crew of beetles soon began doing their stuff on whatever ancient bone was tossed to them. But were they the very same tiny-but-loyal Smithsonian workers? Or has the original crew of the South Yard house been gnawing away quietly on various private projects since the mid-seventies? Who knows?

In 1976, everything happened at once. The National Air and Space Museum opened (three days ahead of schedule!), and the South Yard officially became the Victorian Garden, a beautiful supplement to the newly refurbished Arts and Industries Building. This old Victorian edifice

has become a sort of reincarnation of the Philadelphia Exposition, which celebrated the American Centennial of 1876.

Victoriana reigned both indoors and out. Visitors roamed among wonderfully old-fashioned exhibits in gleaming, wood-frame glass cases, and then stepped out through the west door into the cool, shaded, full-blown elegance of the garden. Even the young felt the tug of a nostalgia they could hardly understand. For in this serene setting from a hundred years ago, they shared sights and sounds, fragrances and feelings that have made real a score of immortal children's stories. They could sense, here, that Alice knew the very same wonders.

The Victorian Garden contained a broad parterre, stretching like a decorative carpet from the central South Door of the Castle to the sidewalk on Independence Avenue, continuing exactly on the axis of L'Enfant Plaza. Its brightly patterned beds and borders changed from season to season. Gravel walks surrounded it and curved away through trees and shrubs. Buds and leaves burgeoned from nineteenth-century urns and cascaded from hanging baskets. Water splashed over a three-tiered fountain and benches invited rest or contemplation. It was a special place.

And all Washington loved it. A tumult of protest exploded when the Smithsonian announced the temporary removal of the Victorian Garden to make way for a nebulous idea, an incredible project for that plot of land. Every reassurance that the garden would reappear was greeted with cynical sneers. No wonder Charles Blitzer, then-Assistant Secretary for History and Art, felt that it had been a "tactical error" of Secretary Ripley's to fashion such a beautiful garden when it was far from permanent.

But plans for a new garden, destined to overlay the three-story sunken structure, were under way. They had been laid well before the tearing up of the tulip beds and the uprooting of all the old trees except the sacrosanct linden.

Carlhian once explained to me a little of his thinking about the garden. "Everyone knows," he said, "that the British are enraptured with gardens. I mean, they're so insular that they consider taking a trip to Italy is 'going abroad,' but they've permeated the world with their notion of the English garden. Traditionally, they saw it as a pocket of 'wild' nature, where one

■ *From left, the south elevation by James Renwick, Jr., circa 1847; earliest lithograph of the south approach to the Castle by Renwick, first published in 1849; the Castle and the U.S. Capitol appear in relation to present-day Independence Avenue in this photograph attributed to Mathew Brady, 1865; a view of the South Yard, circa 1880.*

could walk among beautiful plants and trees: a place of discovery. The French, on the other hand, designed their gardens as extensions of their great buildings. On the landscape they fashioned a series of 'rooms,' perhaps with low walls of shrubbery."

In planning the Haupt Garden, Carlhian and his team set out to blend these two approaches. They kept the Bicentennial parterre. It fitted perfectly with the Victorian aura of the Castle, and lay exactly on its north-south axis, an irresistible benefit in the eyes of any Beaux Arts-trained architect.

"That parterre, the curved walk, and the great linden are intended to evoke the English Victorian garden," Carlhian told me. "The Islamic and oriental gardens, on the east and west, are meant to be extensions of the two pavilions—gardens in the French manner, with axes that carry on the axes of the buildings."

Visitors entering from Independence Avenue and facing the Renwick Gates, built from the same sandstone as was the Castle, would be directly in line with the parterre, and beyond it with the great South Door of the Castle. They would be exactly halfway between the two pavilions. Upon entering either of the pavilions, they would be able to look out upon outdoor rooms, small places for contemplation, each with a meaning.

In designing these, Jean Paul's concern was to forge a link with the theme of the pavilions. He did this by following their motifs, circular for the African, diamond-shaped for the Asian. But he moved each shape *away* from its parent pavilion, the African to the western side of the garden, the Asian to the eastern. This ties the entire composition together.

One of Jean Paul's concerns in the new garden was a round area on the east-west axis between the west door of the Arts and Industries Building and the center of the parterre. What to do with such a spot? It was then that, as he says, "our thoughts began to roam from black African motifs to Islamic. After all, Moslems inhabit North Africa *and* sub-Saharan Africa."

This extension of the theme allowed many new concepts to emerge. S. Dillon Ripley phoned Jean Paul one day and said, "I think the garden should express the history of landscape architecture from Marrakesh to Mindanao." With such enthusiasm to back him, Carlhian set about embellishing his eastern garden spot with an Indian *chadar*—a "water chute" or small waterfall that would ripple down a stone incline. He had the stonework cut in a scallop-like pattern that would add interest to the tumbling water. Little rivulets, then, would be channeled to run right behind the stone benches on which people sat. As Ripley pointed out, on a hot day a visitor could cool off nicely by simply inching back a little.

The chadar fulfilled another requirement, the humdrum duty of concealing the "exhausts" which, according to law, must protrude six feet. Many of the plantings, in fact, serve to hide the skylights and the necessary eight emergency stairways that punctuate the garden—which is, of course, the roof of all the museums, meeting rooms, and offices down below.

The east-west axis continues from the central fountain of the garden adjoining the African Pavilion to the parterre and on. But on the western side, the straight line from the center of the Arts and Industries Building runs into a problem. For the center of the Freer is not on a line with the center door of its old neighbor across the garden. The closest Carlhian could come to finding the axis he sought was to link that Arts and Industries door to the center of the Freer's northern bay—and even that line misses by a few feet.

He saved the situation by running a path from the parterre to another outdoor room, this one a square. From the east, the path enters the square at its southern edge. The path leaves the square from its *northern* edge, and continues, straight and true, to the pair of windows in that north bay of the Freer, a completed axis.

■ *Before being moved to what is now the National Zoological Park, bison lived in the South Yard, far left; the Astrophysical Observatory in 1900; parking dominated the South Yard into the 1970s; the Victorian Garden as it appeared from 1976 to 1983.*

■ *Smithsonian greenhouses maintained hundreds of specimens for planting in the Haupt Garden. Above, gardener trims Podocarpus; opposite, plants labeled for placement.*

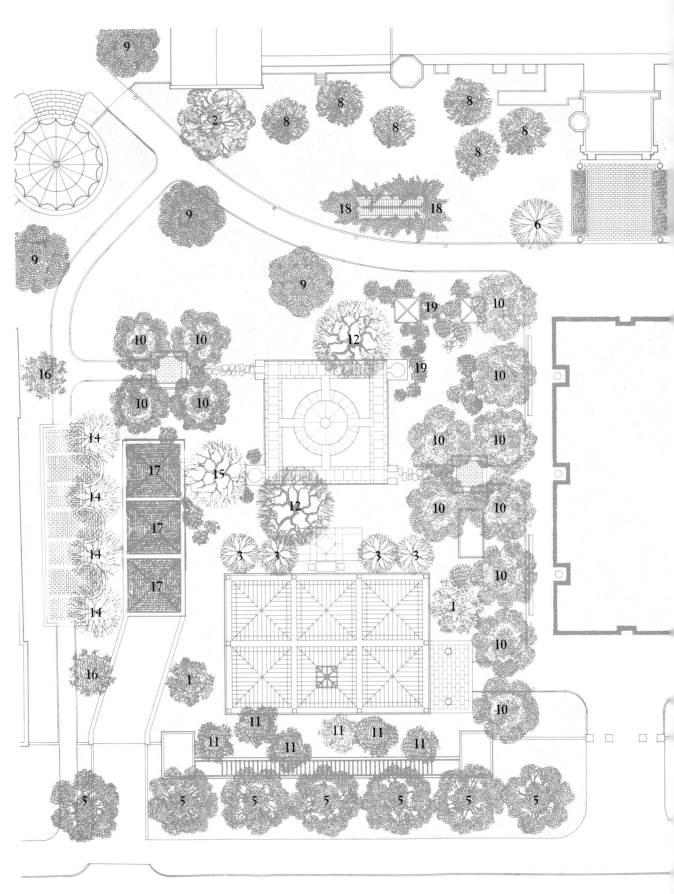

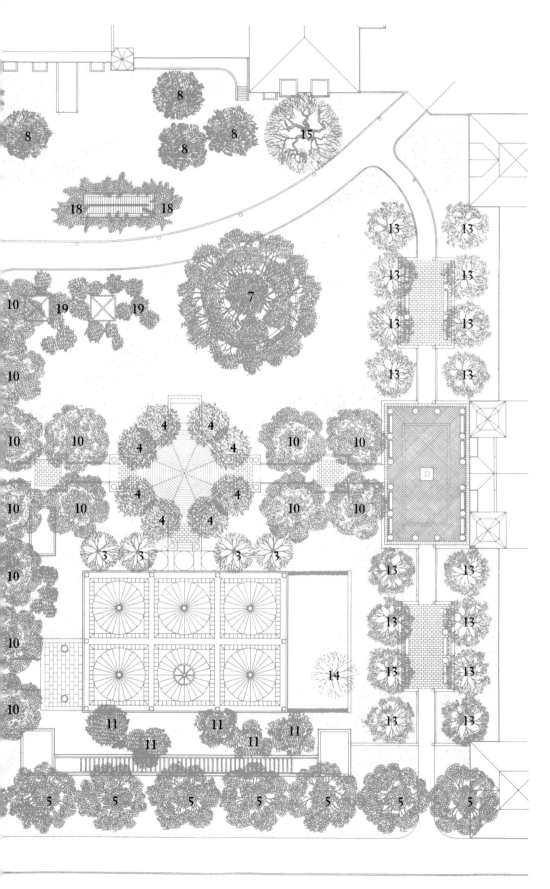

1 (*Acer palmatum* 'Dissectum') / Japanese Threadleaf Maple

2 (*Cedrus libani*) / Cedar of Lebanon

3 (*Cercidiphyllum japonicum*) / Katsura Tree

4 (*Crataegus crus-galli* var. *inermis*) / Thornless Cockspur Hawthorn

5 (*Tilia cordata*) / Little Leaf Linden

6 (*Gingko biloba* "Princeton Sentry") / Princeton Sentry Gingko

7 (*Tilia platyphyllos*) / European Linden

8 (*Ilex opaca*) / American Holly

9 (*Magnolia grandiflora*) / Southern Magnolia

10 (*Magnolia* × *Soulangeana*) / Saucer Magnolia

11 (*Malus* × *Zumi Calocarpa*) / Sargent Crabapple

12 (*Prunus subhirtella* "Pendula") / Weeping Japanese Cherry

13 (*Nyassa sylvatica*) / Sour Gum

14 (*Quercus phellos*) / Willow Oak

15 (*Fagus sylvatica* "Pendula") / Weeping Beech

16 (*Fagus sylvatica* "Fastigiata") / Columnar

17 (*Wisteria floribunda* "Rosea") / Pink Longcluster Wisteria

18 (*Hydrangea petiolaris*) / Climbing Hydrangea

19 *Taxus baccata* "Repandens" / Spreading English Yew

Symmetry and tranquillity mark the moongate garden, above; opposite, landscape architect Lester Collins gestures in discussion with Jean Paul Carlhian; below, seat inspired by the designs of Sir Edwin Lutyens, creator of many famous English gardens.

Carlhian aptly calls this purposeful hitch in his axis a "pinwheel treatment." He made use of his outdoor room to continue that east-west line to its most logical possible conclusion. But the little square area itself has a special beauty. It went through a number of varying concepts. It was almost a plain disk of lawn with a rim of granite seats around it. This was rejected. Carlhian then managed to get a shallow, square pool approved. The pool would enclose a circular stone island in its center, a neat way to transport the African motif westward. The pool is served by four little "causeways," one from each side.

You enter the little square by following that axial pathway and passing through a moongate. This oriental feature is a circular opening in stone, with a straight cut down to the ground. As you go through it, your legs are between the straight walls, your head and torso are within the circular part. Two moongates lead into the square area at two diagonal corners; two others, laid on their sides, form round benches at the other two corners.

West of the square pool, the truck ramp disappears into the innards of the underground building. Its ramp, leading down from Independence Avenue, makes a turn to the right and then back again, hiding the gaping truck entrance—hardly an aesthetic sight, Carlhian feels, from the street. From the garden, you can't see anything of the ramp since high trellises extend over it. They are galvanized steel and wire, densely covered with pink wisteria.

James R. Buckler, Director of the Smithsonian's Office of Horticulture, has a detailed record of the plants and artifacts that have been going into this new garden. He had been gathering a large collection of Victorian garden furnishings—settees and urns—when the old Victorian Garden was curtailed. These are now going back. So are the plants of the parterre.

"Somewhere between forty and forty-five thousand pansies—blue and yellow—were kept in the Smithsonian greenhouses until the parterre was ready for them," he told me. "The furnishings include a great many settees and urns, also lampposts, each with two hanging baskets."

The walks are lined with lampposts separated by a settee or alternately an urn. All are of various nineteenth-century styles, carefully restored at Buckler's facility so they can be used by visitors. You may find yourself resting on a settee with a squirrel motif, or an Egyptian pattern, or a filigreed display of ferns. You may lay your back against iron grapevines or depictions of the four seasons or semireclining wooden slats like those of a rolltop desk. And you may gaze at cast iron Grecian urns or rustic flower stands or vine leaf vases.

"Benches and urns are now extraordinarily costly," said Buckler "so you can see we have a security problem here." For years this magnificent collection has been stored at the Smithsonian greenhouses on the grounds of the National Soldiers' and Airmen's Home in Washington. Visitors to the Arts and Industries Building have seen some of the beautiful benches, tables, chairs, and vases displayed on a balcony above the exhibit of steam-driven engines.

It is due to the generosity of Enid A. Haupt that the new garden exists, and of course she has watched carefully the emergence of its design and the selection of its highly valuable plants and furnishings. Plantings have been dictated by the depth of the soil over the building roof as well as by the various purposes to be served. "Over the roof, depth is about three and a half feet," Jean Paul has noted. Sometimes it's shallower—for example, over the Great Hall and the truck terminal, both of which are open spaces that require thick beams—which, of course, take up space.

"Along Independence Avenue, we'll have a row of littleleaf lindens which will hide the view of the Forrestal Building from people in the garden," said Carlhian. A keyed plan to the garden shows these clearly. They stand about fifteen feet tall and fifteen of them extend along the sidewalk, their line broken only at the Renwick Gates. Entering the gateway, visitors will face the parterre, which is flanked, east and west, by two lines of fourteen saucer magnolias. These eighteen- to twenty-foot trees, their rather heavy leaves offering lots of shade, occur elsewhere in the garden, as backdrops for a series of square sitting areas.

The two pavilions nestle among Sargent crabapples and Katsura trees, also a couple of Japanese threadleaf maples with their wonderfully thick and delicate foliage. Honey locusts and pyramidal European beech help the wisteria shield the truck entrance. Across the garden, beside the Arts and Industries Building, the brick walks lie between two rows of sour

gums, which, growing to about twenty-two feet, are the tallest trees in the garden, aside from the great European linden.

Cockspur thorns surround the circular garden with its chadar. Weeping Japanese cherries droop their branches over the pool of the moongate garden. Near the Kiosk stand a couple of southern magnolias. And along the Castle's south facade are a variety of trees—a cedar of Lebanon, a number of American hollies, a couple of ginkgos that are quite tall, a weeping European beech with its curtain of foliage.

Finally, the entrance to the Castle lies between two beds of roses. Many more plants appear on the chart. And in the greenhouses, flowers have been carefully cultivated for the urns and baskets. The overall feeling of the Enid A. Haupt Garden is of shady serenity produced by a wealth of splendid plantings.

During its early planning stages, Jean Paul Carlhian wrote to garden consultant Lester Collins, a noted landscape architect, "This is a public space, not a private retreat. It is a garden for all seasons. It features open vistas and secluded glens. It is not an arboretum displaying rare species to be gazed at, one by one. Its plant material should be selected for its single statement . . . its symmetrical effect . . . its participation in an overall grouping. . . .

"The garden," he summed up, "should be simple, noble, and grand." ■

■ *Western portal of Arts and Industries Building on perfect axis line with moongate, opposite, left; water in motion typifies the garden adjoining the African Pavilion, below. Chadar is seen behind the fountain. Left, Enid A. Haupt tours the garden with James Buckler, center, and Jean Paul Carlhian.*

On a warm June day in 1983, a trio of expensive, well-polished shoes pressed down on three gleaming, decorative spades, and three small bites appeared in the sod of the Smithsonian's beloved Victorian Garden. Having broken the ground, Vice President George Bush, Chief Justice Warren E. Burger, and Smithsonian Secretary S. Dillon Ripley brushed the soil from their pinstripes and went about their various tasks. The Vice President and the Chief Justice, both representing the Smithsonian Board of Regents, probably put the little ceremony quickly out of mind.

Mr. Ripley, however, was hardly likely to dismiss the significance of what he and his notable companions had wrought. After so long a dream, so intense an effort, his quadrangle project was at last a reality. Three bits of work had suddenly been done on it—tiny, but tangible.

Soon after the groundbreaking came the onslaught. A small army of mud-smeared soldiers in hard hats, armed with gigantic weapons for displacing and reshaping sizable chunks of the earth, mounted their formidable attack. In no time the Victorian Garden was gone and the South Yard of the Castle looked like a piece of no man's land.

Overlooking the battlefield, a double trailer was set up right beside the Castle wall. It was formed from a couple of those prefabricated buildings that you see being trucked along highways with a sign in front warning you of a "Wide Load." For roughly the next four years this nondescript building, so out of place beside its grand Romanesque neighbor, served as headquarters for the field commanders of the quadrangle project. Here the plans were displayed, the paperwork typed up and copied, the staff meetings held. The place became almost as much a part of the Smithsonian as the old outbuildings that predated the garden.

I learned to feel quite at home in the trailer. Here I would meet Jean Paul Carlhian and peer over his shoulder at the architectural plans. Here I would listen to the debates about the feasibility of time schedules. Here I would feel depressed by reports of unforeseen problems and elated by their solution. Here hung the hard hats for our wear in the trenches outside, and here we'd scrape the mud off our shoes when we returned from the front.

■ *The Castle looms above the growing excavation, opposite; right, ground-breaking on June 21, 1983. Secretary Ripley looks on as Chief Justice Warren Burger, left, and Vice President George Bush share a congratulatory handshake.*

■ *Construction engineer Charlie Putnam, above; right, three underground levels in varying stages of construction. At center, trailer headquarters for project managers.*

Charlie Putnam held down the most visited office inside the trailer, and in the course of the construction I talked with him many times. He's construction engineer for the General Services Administration, the government branch that supervises construction projects that make use of government funds. Half the funding for this project, remember, came from the federal government. The Smithsonian raised the other half.

Way back at the very beginning—the beginning of the world, it seems—the General Services Administration awarded the contract to Blake Construction Company as the lowest bidder in the required public offering. Blake, in turn, subcontracted with other outfits for specialized jobs on the project. And always Charlie Putnam sat at his unpretentious desk in the trailer and somehow managed to keep tabs on everything that was going on. For four long years he held the project together and kept it moving forward.

Charlie, who hails from Millboro, Virginia, is a tall, athletic man with a moustache and a pleasant and often colorful country-southern way of speaking. A graduate of Virginia Polytechnic Institute, Charlie is the veteran of many GSA projects. He's been field commander of this campaign ever since those three brass hats with the gilded spades kicked it off, and he's learned to implement Jean Paul Carlhian's creative ideas, and sometimes blow the whistle on them when they won't work.

Without question, Charlie Putnam knows more about how to dig a 4.2-acre, sixty-foot-deep hole right next to a sacrosanct Castle without sending it crashing into the excavation than any other man in the whole wide world.

According to Charlie, the crash of the Castle was, because of stringent precautions, never even a remote, unthinkable possibility. Yet. . . . "The South Tower once sank almost an inch and a half," he told me, "but we managed to stabilize things before we lost the whole building." He said it quietly, without drama or emotion, the way an old Marine sergeant talks about taking Mount Suribachi back in forty-five. I pressed him, and kneaded him, and finally worked out of him the story of the Smithsonian's own Battle of the Big Hole.

"Our problem was to make the excavation without rocking the Castle, or the Arts and Industries Building, or the Freer," said Charlie. "And the only way we could do it was to use slurry walls. You know about slurry walls?"

Well, not really, but I soon learned. When you have to dig a deep hole you must shore up the walls as you go down, right? The usual way to do this is to slam huge upright steel beams down into the ground, one after the other, to form a steel sheath for your excavation. But as every city office worker knows, that endless hammering right across the street often makes your desk twitch and your typewriter jump, and the snapshot of your family on last summer's vacation fall on the floor. So imagine what it might do to a fragile sandstone building right on the edge of the site, a structure whose foundations are difficult to find (the Castle's

cornerstone never *has* been found), much less reinforce.

Instead of using those steel beams, what about a concrete retaining wall? That would safeguard your excavation, but you'd need to dig a deep trench around the site to shore up the concrete that was to hold back the earth before you poured in the concrete. And the trouble is, when you have to go as deep as sixty feet, the walls of your trench will collapse inward before you finish and get the concrete into it.

That problem, however, has been licked. French engineers have developed a technique to hold trench walls in place while you're still digging. They would mix a thick soup (trust the French!) of water and bentonite, a kind of clay. Then, using a narrow trenching shovel, a "clamshell," they'd scoop earth out of the trench, replacing it, all the while, with this slurry soup. The slurry would hold the earthen walls in place.

This was the most feasible way to build a retaining wall for the excavation, while saving the Castle and the other museum buildings on the site from damage. The trench would be dug in sections, the slurry filling up what the clamshells took out. As each section was finished, concrete would be fed into it from the bottom up, and the slurry would be pushed up to the surface and ejected. And presto! You'd have your concrete wall with nary a bang nor a quiver to disturb the surroundings.

At the Smithsonian, bids went out from Blake Construction Company, and two firms were awarded subcontracts: Griffin De-Watering and a

■ *Pouring the slurry,* left; *near right, workers guide reinforcing cage into the hole; far right, tiebacks line the slurry wall; below, tieback loading equipment.*

French company, Intra-For-Cofor. "The French were anxious to get into the American market with their slurry walls," and, said Charlie, "they figured on using French personnel.

"But the union made them pay an American wage and use Americans as operators of the equipment. So we had a training problem. The local crane operators had trouble using those clamshells because they couldn't see them, way down there in the trench. They had to learn to do everything by feel."

Learning took so long that eventually the union allowed the experienced French operators to do the excavating. Gradually the work progressed. But the sea of troubles took a long time to cross. The French engineers and operators knew little English; the Americans knew no French. "I went to a meeting in New York," Charlie recalled. "Wall-to-wall engineers, including French structural experts. It was hard enough for me to understand what any of them were talking about any of the time, but when the French started in with their technical stuff it seemed hopeless."

An engineer from Griffin De-Watering, the American subcontractor, managed to work out a sort of communication system with the French, and served as interpreter. Without him, said Charlie, "Lord knows. . . ."

Panel by panel, the trench around the quadrangle went down, the slurry went in, prefabricated sections of reinforcing cage were lowered into the soup, then concrete gushed down through a sixty-foot "tremie" pipe and the slurry burbled out the top. The concrete then hardened and you had a wall. But, as Charlie pointed out, as soon as you dug your excavation beside it, the outside pressure of the ground would collapse that wall in no time.

So to hold the wall intact, the engineers used tiebacks. I remembered seeing them piled on the site—long bundles of cable-like steel rods, each bundle surrounding a sixty-foot plastic pipe. For about half its length the pipe had a series of perforations. The idea is to drill a sixty-foot hole through the concrete retaining wall and on into the earth, slanting down at about a twenty-degree angle. You fill the hole with slurry as you go down. Then you replace the slurry with grout—two parts cement to one part water, which Charlie says has the consistency of Pepto Bismol. Before the grout sets, you ram a bundle of rods, with that perforated pipe in the middle of them, down into the claggy hole. The perforated end goes in first.

Now you have to wait until the grout sets around that strange, sixty-foot gathering of rods and pipe. When that happens, you feed more grout, under tremendous pressure, through the plastic pipe. When it reaches a set of perforations this stuff blasts through them and balloons out into the earth to form corrugated concrete balls at intervals. And so, far underground, each tieback blossoms with these bulbous anchors.

When a tieback is solidly in place, you grasp it mechanically at each wall panel, and you pull it tight—and I mean some kind of *tight*—and lock it off. And as they say, "That there wall ain't goin' to walk *anywhere*."

Well, that's what they say. Actually, the retaining wall right beside the Castle took a tiny step inward when some tiebacks failed to hold after the great excavation was finished. The anchors gave just a hair, and that was enough to produce, magically, a number of sudden cracks in the plaster of various Castle rooms.

"That was kind of scary," Charlie said. "We'd set up instruments to check for movement in the walls at all the buildings around the quadrangle, and we'd been monitoring them once a week. Now we increased the readings to one a day, and a survey crew came in to check their accuracy. We found the Castle had sunk an inch and three-eighths."

There was no way to bring it back. But the sag hadn't damaged it, and

the work crews excavated the area around the South Tower and stabilized it by drilling down and setting in pin piles and additional tiebacks. "Those cracks—and some in the Freer—were the only way you'd know what had happened," Charlie said.

All the tiebacks stayed in the retaining walls until the three floors of the building were in place. With the floor slabs all complete and exerting their pressure against the inside of the retaining walls, the tiebacks could be detentioned or the load released by burning off the anchor plates on the inside face of the slurry wall.

Doing this phase of the project, one workman was almost blown off his scaffold because his acetylene torch set off some gas that had gathered in the tieback hole. "It may have penetrated an old sewer," Charlie told me. "Maybe something dead. Anyway, the flame shot out of there like it was a gun barrel, and it scared the hell out of everybody. From then on we used sniffers when we went to loosen the tiebacks."

Try as I might, I couldn't help but conjure up a dead dinosaur as the source of the gas. The Monster of the Quad. Dead since the Mesozoic, its gases mysteriously trapped in a capsule of clay, impermeable until a tieback violated it. After all, during the excavation of the Big Hole, a log of wood was uncovered right down at the sixty-foot level. A paleontologist from the Museum of Natural History identified it as bald cypress, and from its cell walls the lab people gave it an age—29,000 years, plus or minus a few decades.

I remember going to see that log when it was found. It had been squeezed and deformed by the pressure of all that clay on top of it, but you could still see the tree rings. The paleontologist figures that it sank in still water, in a bay of the Potomac, which meandered all over the Washington area at the end of the last Ice Age.

This piece of bald cypress got waterlogged and ended up on a hard, sandy bottom, with centuries of silt drifting down on it. The silt turned to clay—lots of pressure, but soft—so the top of the log kept its rounded shape. The bottom was pressed flat, however. And since no oxygen reached the log, it stayed that way until a summer day in 1984. I still have a little piece of it.

I remember noticing, down in the hole that time, a little seepage from

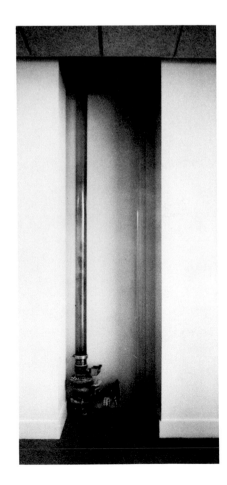

the retaining walls. That presence of water was always one of the tricky problems that faced Charlie Putnam and his people. "From the start, we had to control the ground water," he told me. "Our excavation, remember, went down about twenty-five feet deeper than the ground water level."

How in the world, I wondered, could an excavation go below that water level? It turns out that the excavators controlled the water with seventeen "well points," places outside the perimeter of the Big Hole. At these points, they sank eight-inch pipes far below the water level, and turned on a battery of pumps to drain the water away.

"We burned an awful lot of juice keeping those pumps going," Charlie said. "And when we had a couple of floors in, I asked if we could cut them out and let the outside water come back around the retaining walls. The experts said, 'No way.' They told me I had to wait until the roof was on. Otherwise the building would tend to float."

When, finally, the roof was in place, the pumps were shut off, and everyone waited for the water level to rise around the building. Oddly enough, it came back far slower than anyone thought it would. "We'd planned to wait for it to return to where it had been, and then check the seams between the retaining wall panels for leaks. But it came back so slowly—about a half-inch a day—that we couldn't wait. We dug out *all* the old seams, whether they needed it or not, and then jammed grout in under high pressure so that all the crevices and cracks were filled."

Charlie said he didn't know why the water was so reluctant to come back. I wondered, of course, if the lost water table proved that civilization was drying up, but he wouldn't be drawn into substantiating such a hot news story. He said maybe the digging of the Washington Metro had something to do with it.

He asked if I'd like another look at the building, and of course I said yes. We left the trailer and needed to walk only a few steps through the dust or mud (I don't remember which, but it was always one or the other) before reaching one of the emergency stairways that lead down into the earth. Now they're camouflaged by garden plants. Back then, the garden hadn't been started.

On the lowest level of the building, Charlie showed me an upright pipe of solid—and very strong—glass. It starts from the floor and goes up into the ceiling, where, he told me, it forms a gooseneck. It was completely filled with water. "That's how the water table is monitored," Charlie said. "You just check the level in the glass pipe."

While we were about it, we also checked a seam in an exposed portion of the retaining wall, far below ground. We could find no tiny, telltale trickle. Just dry, knobbly concrete.

Workers were painting, setting tile or carpet on the floors, putting in wiring and switches. I found myself bursting with impatience to have it all over with, at last. Always, there seem to be so many small, frustrating delays at the very end of a building project.

"Do you want to see some more?" Charlie asked.

"I just want to see it finished," I said.

"So do I," he said.

The last major chore the contractors faced, after the roof of the complex was in place, was to get the garden soil on top of it. It came from the bottom of the Potomac, dredged from around the General Services Administration power plant. It was trucked to the University of Maryland and, in Charlie's words, "tested all to hell" before being dumped on the roof.

It lay there in mindless heaps, and I looked at it when we emerged again from the stairway. "Is it good soil?" I asked.

"Best in the world. It's been growing clover you wouldn't believe. Wait till you see it go to work on Jim Buckler's plants."

Already the soil was producing an extravagant crop of weeds as it lay heaped amid the rubble of the Big Hole. I wished the last scraps of masonry and lumber, the last rusted, unused tie rod and broken sack of cement, the last paper cup and cigarette butt were gone, and the soil was in place in its berms and swales, and the trees and flowers were taking root in the richness of it.

By the side of what would one day be a garden path, an iron lamppost lay on its side next to an upright pipe. The pipe, I was told, rose from a whole system of pipes that had been buried underground. All carried the power lines that would feed electricity to the lamps. They were all in place, ready to be hooked up and turned on.

Charlie turned back toward the trailer. "Anything else I can help you with?" he asked.

I shook my head. He wanted to get back to work, finishing the building, and I wasn't about to stop him. ∎

Glass pipe on Concourse level monitors the water table, opposite; above, tons of earth exited the Big Hole via the truck ramp.

133

On one of my first visits to the site of the Smithsonian's new museum complex, while construction was under way, I noticed a small piece of masonry that I had never seen before, anywhere. It was a slab of limestone about two inches thick, that somehow formed a ninety-degree angle. How in the world, I wondered, had that been done? Can you *bend* limestone around a corner? Can you *mold* it into that sharp angle? Everything seems to be possible, these days, but still. . . .

My guide, Jean Paul Carlhian, was overjoyed at my puzzlement. "It is traditional to make corners out of two pieces, no? But this is not a traditional building. So these corners are one piece, cut as you see, in this manner."

That was my introduction to the project's standard of excellence. To maintain it, Carlhian has traveled extensively, argued strenuously, irritated the builders necessarily, and found, fortuitously, craftsmen who met his demands.

The search for excellence started with the choice of materials for the new structure. "The pavilions," said Carlhian, "had to fit visually between the granite of the Freer, the red brick of the Arts and Industries Building, and the reddish brown sandstone of the Castle. We were not going to allow the pavilions to look like a baby Freer and a baby A and I, you know, so we needed something different that wouldn't fight with the existing buildings."

Durability was the first major factor. The material should be granite. But what color? Carlhian said he always thought of Africa as pink and Asia as green. "I knew of some greenish granite in the Baltic states, and got hold of a sample which I rather liked. But the building committee was horrified. Green granite, indeed! So I kept looking through the samples in my office."

Carlhian decided on a grayish color with pink in it, called Rockville Beige, for the Sackler Pavilion—on the west side of the quadrangle. This stone would harmonize with the Arts and Industries Building on the eastern side of the quadrangle, and so tie the structures together visually, west to east. This choice won approval. He then set about finding a stone

Pale blue glass subtly filters staircase light in the African Pavilion.

■ *Ascending the pavilion staircases.*
Right, Sackler Gallery; opposite, African
Art. Across top, features of building ex-
teriors.

for the African Pavilion—on the eastern side of the quadrangle—which would reflect the warm tones of the Freer and so provide the same visual cross-tie, east to west.

Jean Paul went to Cold Spring, Minnesota, to see the stone he had chosen. It's a smallish town in the center of the state, not far from the infant Mississippi River. He remembers that it was very cold. But he was warmed by a small, friendly organization where generations of stoneworkers had proved their skill through the years. One of the first things he noticed at the plant was a stack of the very same granite that he'd wanted for the African Pavilion. "It had been shipped up from the quarry so the Cold Spring people could work on it. It needed some delicate cutting, and this was the place for it."

Seeing it now, Jean Paul realized the stone contained too much quartz. "It was too sparkly for what I wanted." So he journeyed down to the Texas quarries that had produced it, and there found a granite called "Sunset Red" that filled the bill.

On one of his trips to Texas, Carlhian noticed a great number of small round granite disks piled carelessly aside, and was intrigued with them. They were, it turned out, the residue from a masonry process that was being used at the quarry in the shaping of tombstones. They were the cores of circular drillings and were simply lying around waiting for someone to find a use for them.

"They looked like hockey pucks," said Jean Paul, "and they gave me an idea for the bottom of a pool in the garden. We had wanted something that would have the texture to catch snow in winter, so that when the pool was drained the bottom would still look nice. It seemed to me that these hockey pucks, set on edge, would give the bottom an interesting wavy look."

But a pool would require hundreds of them, and only the tops would show. So how about cutting them in half? Doing so would eke them out, and also simplify the project. Only the round edges would show; the unpolished cut edges would be set in the pool bottom.

The quarriers were delighted to make the needed cuts and polishes. Carlhian's half hockey pucks were drawn into the garden plan. Set in a staggered formation, they provide an even, rippled texture, pleasing to the eye, especially when snow lies between the little round bumps and etches them.

The granite for the exterior of the pavilions needed different finishes: polished, sanded, rubbed. Around the windows and doors is a band of highly polished stone, glassy smooth. Under the copper roofs the stone is rough, so it will pick up the greenish stain of the copper's patina. When the copper domes and pyramids first went up, Carlhian asked many of his friends whether they wanted the patina or the polished copper look— which is very nice. Having known from the beginning that a patina was planned, I had made up my mind to like it, and I told this to Jean Paul.

He looked up anxiously at the bright roofs. "I wish the patina would hurry, then," he said. "Perhaps we should have used the urine of a pregnant mare."

"What?" I asked, not unnaturally.

"You're supposed to paint copper with the urine of a pregnant mare to get a good patina quickly," he told me. "Everyone knows that."

Anyway, if and when the patina arrives, with or without thanks to the mare in question, the architect wants the stain to creep down the granite of the pavilions' top courses. These, then, must be rough. The rest of the outer walls have a medium finish.

"Two prominent pieces went into a pavilion wall with too high a polish," Carlhian recalled. "I had to tell the builders that they were unacceptable, and of course the builders weren't very pleased. Construction engineer Charlie Putnam told me that he and his people had checked every single piece that had gone into the building about twenty times and nobody had noticed anything wrong. I said I was sorry, but the pieces *were* wrong, and no doubt about it, and they'd have to be sent back to Cold Spring.

"But before they started on the terrible job of removing the pieces, Putnam called Cold Spring and told them about the mistake. They sent a team of experts who roughened the high polish on those pieces while they were in place. That was a wonderful firm to work with."

Jean Paul wanted people to appreciate the specialness of the pavilions, so he wouldn't allow his granite to be cut in the usual pieces of thin veneer that you find on most industrial buildings. The external slabs are

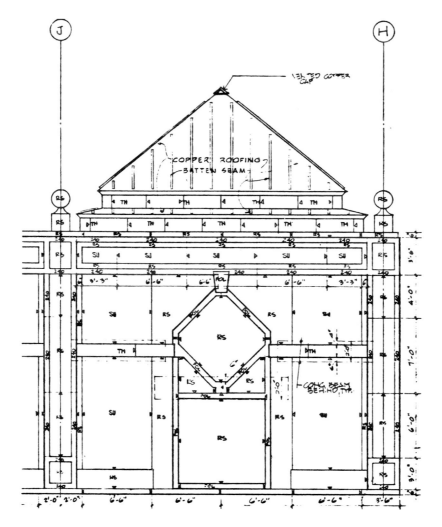

at least two inches thick—about three times the thickness of veneer. Also, new stone-cutting processes allowed the granite to be cut in huge sheets. Carlhian says the Cold Spring people offered to make the round windows of the African Pavilion by simply cutting them out of a solid wall of granite. They'd then throw away the inside of the circle, and as Jean Paul said, "That was going too far."

But he did want the sense of solidity that big pieces gave the buildings. "I didn't want the pavilions to look like Madison Avenue perfume stores," he said. So he called for sanded granite walls, to get away from the polished look, and highly polished granite window frames to avoid the use of metal.

Metal inside, however, was another matter. "I wanted the metal frames and stairway balustrades to have the look of ancient bronze—the sort of look you get at Pompeii. But you can't paint that look, at least in a solid color. Then I found exactly what I wanted in a balustrade in Cambridge, at MIT. With this inspiration, Bob Holloran devised a way to spray blue, green, and gold with a high-pressure nozzle, and we used it to give the high balustrade its special look—mottled aqua, flecked with gold streaks."

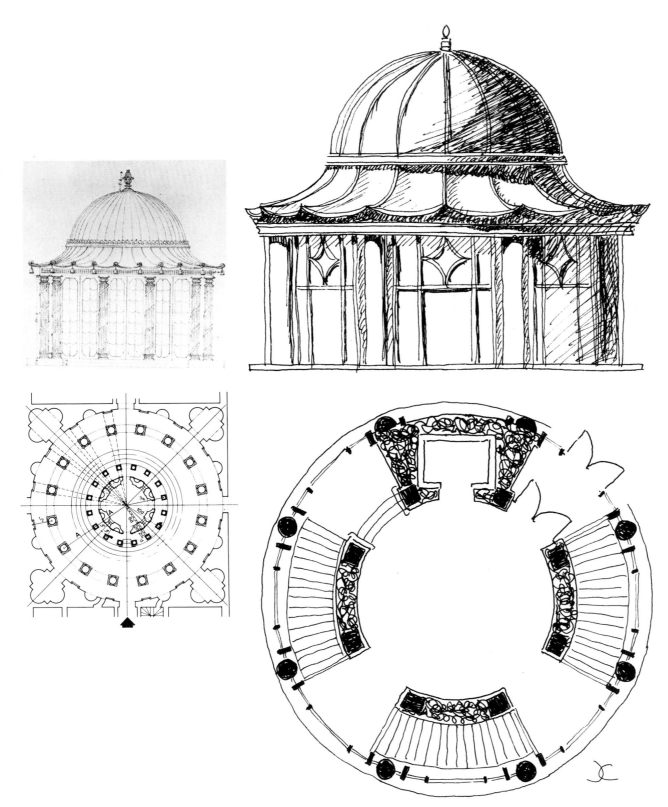

■ Precedents: *Architect Carlhian shows derivations for the Kiosk. Wanting something "gay and playful," he thought of this nineteenth-century design for a conservatory by G. S. Repton, upper left. Below is the plan of Bramante's tempietto of St. Peter in Montorio in Rome. Exterior view of the Kiosk and its entry level plan are at right.*

Below the balustrade is the handrail that the law requires for the handicapped. This was plain bronze, to be smoothed and brightened by the rubbing of hands.

What of the Kiosk, the entrance for staff and for the public attending classes, lectures, and International Center exhibitions? It stands small and bright at the northwest corner of the garden, and you might think it would be overlooked in the company of the elegant pavilions. But Jean Paul loves the Kiosk.

"It isn't oriental or African, but just itself," he once remarked. "It's really a sort of conning tower for the building below, but I decided to give it the personality of a bandstand in a park. That meant it should be light and white, to look like wood. And that meant using limestone. We found what we wanted—plain, unblemished limestone, off-white on the warm side—in Indiana, and I asked that the columns be cut in big, single pieces, shaped to wrap around the structural columns. It was hard to do, but the Indiana people did it. My main thought was to emulate the quality and workmanship of the National Gallery of Art."

Carlhian scalloped the edge of the Kiosk dome and repeated the shape in the building's windows and stonework. A scallop is a combination of a diamond and a circle, and this shape recalls the roof line of the Castle's adjoining tower as well as relating to the circles and angles of the two pavilions.

■ *Work in progress viewed from Independence Avenue shows the Kiosk's precise position between the Freer Gallery and the Castle.*

The intricacy of copper plating on the Kiosk's dome sets a standard of craftsmanship, right. Opposite, the completed building.

The Kiosk needed to house an elevator, a reception desk, a circular stairwell, and lots of light. So glass walls allow light to flood into the Kiosk and the limestone, cut in huge pieces, reflects the light and carries it downward as far as possible.

Going down the circular stairway, beside the limestone core of the Kiosk, I had the experience of being told something I absolutely had never heard of before. At my age this is remarkable, because although there are myriad things I don't understand, I've heard of most of them. We had started down the stairs, keeping to the right of the stairway, holding the rail there. And Jean Paul paused and turned and said, "You'd be surprised at how many beginning architects forget about the circular stairway rule."

"What in the world are you talking about?" I asked.

"A circular stairway must always descend counter-clockwise, at least in this country. And most others. And of course that means it goes up clockwise. . . ."

I stared at him, astonished.

"You see? You are as bad as my young beginners. Look," he placed his foot on the step below him. "The tread here is wide enough for my whole foot, and when I step down I place my whole foot on it. If I'm going *up* . . . you see? I step up with just my toes. And so I use the tread at the inside of the stair, where it's narrow. For just my toes, it's wide enough. Try it. So! Now you see that when people are used to right-hand traffic, this is the way the circular stairway must be designed. In Britain, I do not know."

It took a while, but I worked it out.

The copper dome of the Kiosk is made of individual squares of copper to give it the look of, in Carlhian's words, "the skin of a mermaid." It too will achieve a warm, serene patina. Carlhian indicated that copper has been much cheaper in the mid-eighties than for some years.

The wood that provides corridor and vestibule flooring in the Sackler is oak. Carlhian's architectural teammate, Robert Holloran, discovered it in Georgia, a fine stack of unblemished white oak that had been bought up by a bonding company. Oak also enhances doorways in both museums and beautifies elevators.

The glass in the north side of the pavilions is triple glazed and clear. Carlhian wanted people to be able to look out northward on the garden. The light would be behind them and directly on the plants and trees of the scene outside.

The glass people made each window in a single piece. Intricate work went to a firm in Roxbury, just outside downtown Boston, where, again, all the usual rules were broken so that the Smithsonian would get exactly what the architect wanted.

The architect also wanted windows on the Independence Avenue side so that, in his words, "people walking along there would realize that these pavilions are living buildings, not just monuments. Since these south-facing windows would take in a lot of sunlight, I thought perhaps they should be tinted blown glass to have a filtering effect. Mr. Ripley suggested I have a look at the tomb of Marshal Foch in Paris. So I did. And I saw the tombs of the other military heroes of France, all around Foch's, and all were touched by the faint amber look from amber-tinted glass. I thought it was a wonderful idea."

Carlhian wanted amber glass in the Sackler Pavilion, a blue tint in the African. A glance at the Afterword to this book explains why some changes were made. But Jean Paul's intention, he remembers, was that "in the evening the sun will pick up shadows of the pavilion stairways—one angling around its stairwell, one circling it—and cast shadows on the limestone walls. There will be the little tint, blue in one pavilion, amber in the other, not like what you see in a church, but nonetheless adding a certain quality to the light. And as the sun travels, the pattern will change, subtly. And after dark, people hurrying along Independence Avenue will see the soft light from those blown glass windows and know that this is a special place." ■

International Center

The International Center, an exhibition and public education facility on the Concourse level of the museum complex, is the primary site for the Smithsonian's international programs that include exhibitions, films, performances, lectures, conferences, public forums, and workshops. International Center programs are designed to promote greater cultural and scientific understanding of peoples and regions of the world, with particular emphasis on the cultures and land of the Americas.

Smithsonian National Associate Program

Since its inception in 1970, the Smithsonian National Associate Program has provided innovative educational opportunities for Smithsonian Associates throughout the nation. Through *Smithsonian* magazine, Associates participate in activities that increase their awareness of the Institution and which encourage support for its work.

The National Associate Program now serves more than two million members and is comprised of a lecture and seminar program, a travel program, and a contributing membership program.

Smithsonian Resident Associate Program

Established in 1965, and receiving no federal funding, the largely self-supporting program is a vital and active link between the Institution and the metropolitan Washington community. It offers a broad range of quality educational and cultural activities that enhance appreciation of the collections, exhibitions, and research of the Institution as well as consonant activities of timely interest. Over 270,000 people attend more than two thousand activities each year; membership has grown from eight thousand in 1972 to nearly sixty thousand today.

Smithsonian Institution Traveling Exhibition Service (SITES)

SITES was founded in 1952 as a Smithsonian resource for other museums, and has since grown into the largest and most diverse traveling exhibition service in America. The shows span a range of subjects—art, science, technology, history, design, ethnic studies, and popular culture. In any given year, SITES exhibitions visit virtually every state in the Union, nearly all of Canada's provinces, locations throughout Mexico—in fact, "sites" the world over. SITES shows are seen by nearly seven million people annually.

Education Center

The Education Center, a pan-Institution facility, occupies all the classrooms and the auditorium on the north side of the Concourse. Funding for its construction was generously provided by the Pew Memorial Trust.

Perhaps the most vital area of the underground structure, the place that renders it habitable for humans and treasures alike, is an area that few will ever see. Thanks to my association with construction engineer Charlie Putnam, I did see it—the vast mechanical equipment room on the lowest level of the building. Two stories high, it stretches for the entire length from east to west along the building's Independence Avenue side.

Visitors and staff may notice—but possibly not—the absolutely constant temperature and humidity in the building. The need for it is obvious, but the method of obtaining this uniform environment isn't. You really have to know Charlie to see how it's done.

The mechanical room hums with the endless spinning of nine huge fan units. Massive rotary supply fans send air in every direction, all through the structure from pavilions to distant classrooms. Across a walkway from each one, the return unit sucks air back to be reconditioned. "Most buildings cut off all outside air when it gets very cold," said Charlie. "Not here. At least 10 percent of the air is fresh, brought in from the outside, even on the coldest day."

These great units were installed in the building while there was still an open area above, through which they could be lowered. Once in, they couldn't be removed without being disassembled. So before installation, they had to prove they could meet the design criteria. They were tested at the plant where they were built, in Mississippi.

Charlie Putnam and a crew he took to Mississippi stood over the testing process, improved the methods, and failed three units. It took four months or so for them to be deemed satisfactory for the Smithsonian.

Now the units circulate the air, returning it to be chilled or heated by water or steam. The water is from Washington's city system, but each chiller has its own pumping system down in the mechanical room. Steam comes from the central steam plant run by the General Services Administration. Temperature, 74 degrees, and humidity, 50 percent, are monitored constantly by control instrumentation throughout the building. Data gathering panels note the readings and transmit them to a central computer system in the Natural History Building across the Mall. The

■ *Architect Carlhian calls this part of the Concourse the "Green Room."*

computer makes the decisions about keeping the environment exactly even—as it must be for the sake of the invaluable collections.

Down in this great room is the telephone room and a central power switchboard with hand switches the size of an emergency brake and a generator that kicks in automatically in case of a power failure. A tangle of copper piping eight inches in diameter sprouts from a pumping complex to feed water to the fountains in the garden and the Concourse.

Everything here is new, and works, and is the best. "It's the state of the art. All of it," said Charlie Putnam.

So is the rest of the museum complex. Take the business of designing with regard to city vistas and lines connecting centers of existing buildings. This is one of Jean Paul Carlhian's subtle strengths, and only after months do I see these axes before being told where to look for them. Now I see them everywhere.

Especially at night. I think many of us share a habit of lining up shapes, of noticing matching angles, of finding visual parallels. And if we waken for some reason at three in the morning, we don't succumb to the panicky realization that our lost sleep may cripple our efforts to solve tomorrow's problems, meet its schedules, make its decisions. Instead, we lie still and stare at patterns on the ceiling—shadows of window frames, etched by street lights, the triangle formed by a half-open closet door.

After working beside Jean Paul Carlhian for many months, I'm convinced that all architects are insomniacs who bisect the angles on their nighttime ceilings, who find strange uses for the shapes that appear in the gloom of their walls and doorways. For that is what he sees, and I now do, too, as we walk through his building.

He pauses in the Sackler Pavilion and points at the central garden door, facing the Castle. "Isn't that nice?" he asks. I thought, the first time he said this, that he meant just the entrance with its diagonal motif, and I simply nodded agreement, wondering why such an eminent architect needed to have his ego bolstered. But the second time, I realized that he

■ *Although climate control equipment dominates this view of the massive mechanical room, the complex actually requires less equipment than would an aboveground building of comparable size.*

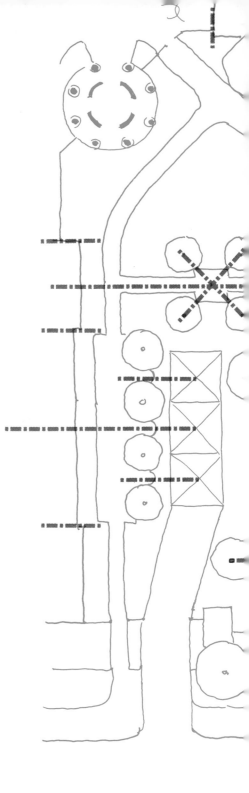

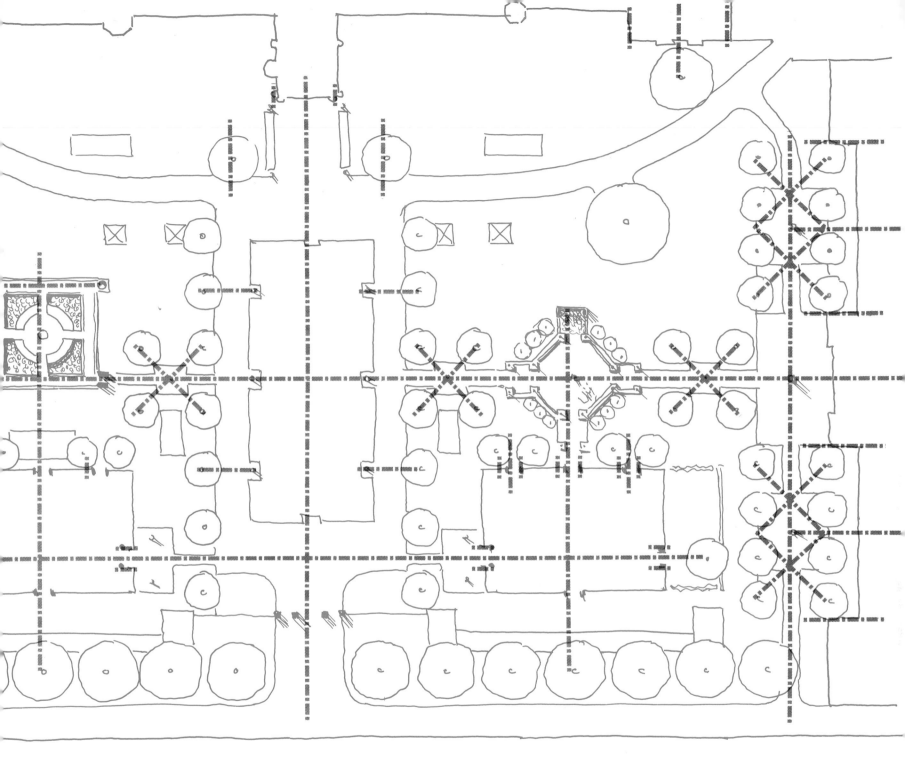

■ In this drawing, Carlhian shows the overall design organization of the site, which is based on the crossing of two axes. The north-south axis extends southward from the Castle and maintains L'Enfant's original planned extension on 10th Street toward the Potomac.

The east-west axis is based upon the west entrance to the Arts and Industries Building.

was indicating the shapes you see *through* that particular opening. For this central doorway neatly frames a similar central element, a doorway in the Castle with a small set of steps leading up to it. This occurs directly under the Castle's South Tower, and the pyramidal shape of the transom above that pavilion door frames and repeats the angles of that tower roof.

The plan repeats the same visual game again and again. In the Enid A. Haupt Garden, every lane between lines of trees ends at a meaningful point, the center of a bay of the Freer or the Arts and Industries Building. One east-west axis runs into the huge trellis that conceals the truck ramp. And next time you're waiting for the light to change so you can cross Independence Avenue and walk up L'Enfant Plaza, take a second or two to look the other way. For as you stand directly in line with the center of the plaza, you are also on a line that accurately bisects the Renwick Gates, the parterre of the Haupt Garden, and, beyond, the South Door of the Castle. Three levels underground, that same north-south line cuts right through the central fountain of the Concourse and the tall arched mirrors on each side of it.

The garden trees will grow and the plantings will change with the seasons, but those architectural lines, those axes, will always remain. So will the motifs of the two pavilions and the Kiosk, though the buildings may seem almost to sink behind the grassy berms and burgeoning flora that surround them.

Though the brutal heat of summer, the windblown snow and crackling cold of winter will gradually weather the granite and limestone of the buildings, those stone window frames will always be glossier than the broad, thick slabs of the walls. The unseamed columns and one-piece

corners will always astonish and delight those who seek (and seldom find) quality.

The copper roofs of the pavilions will turn green and become unobtrusive amid the foliage of the growing trees, but always, for those who pause to look at them, their shapes, domed, pyramidal, and in the case of the Kiosk a little of both, will somehow seem subtly fitting.

People may wonder why those shapes feel right. And then, as though they were lying awake, staring at the shadows on a ceiling, their eyes will travel from the domes of the African Pavilion to the rounded bays of the Freer and the Romanesque arches of the Castle. And from the angles of the Sackler Pavilion to the gables and roof lines of the Arts and Industries Building. And whether or not they consciously see the repeated shapes, they will sense a unity and a satisfaction.

People—thousands of them—will, as the years pass, walk through the underground galleries and absorb the glories of the collections on display. And if they pause at the bottom of the pavilion stairs and look back, they will see the shapes that the stairways take, rounded or angular, and the shadows that spring from them as they wrap around that welcome shaft of light, pouring downward from the distant skylight, penetrating ninety feet to the reflecting pool, bathing the entire stairwell.

Whatever marvels enchant the sightseers, whatever duties absorb the staff workers, whatever new learning excites the students, all will be aware of the basic plan calling for light and air. The architect provided elements that remove the sense of underground oppression, that turn the whole complex within the quadrangle over to human beings as an environment in which to linger, a place to visit again and again. ∎

■ *In the seven years of its association with the quadrangle project, Shepley, Bulfinch, Richardson and Abbott made 489 drawings. Only this one, however, shows the project completed.*

This book attempts to tell the story of how an extraordinary edifice was planned and built under strange and difficult conditions. Before the book was completed, the difficulties increased. The underground museum complex beneath the two pavilions underwent such alterations that it no longer adheres to the design described in these pages.

What in the world happened?

Writing in the *New York Times*, William Rubin, Director of the Department of Painting and Sculpture at the Museum of Modern Art, pointed out examples of art museums where the architecture overwhelms the content. "Is it possible," asked Rubin, "that the greater the architect—the more personal, original and forceful his vision—the more problematic his spaces will be for exhibiting painting and sculpture?"

Rubin cited the New National Gallery of Berlin, by architect Mies van der Rohe, and Frank Lloyd Wright's Guggenheim, in New York, both masterpieces of architecture, as "among the museums *least* suited to showing the art for which they were created." He mentioned Washington's East Wing of the National Gallery, that dramatic creation of I. M. Pei, as having such vast display spaces "that Brobdingnagian works had to be specially ordered for it."

As Jean Paul Carlhian's quadrangle project was being completed, a number of Smithsonian museum people began to feel that it, similarly, would prove too grand, too lavish, too apt to distract attention from the special impact of the Sackler and African Art collections that would go into it. Memos began to fly. Museum planners sought various modifications: Eliminate the planned coffered ceilings because coffers would get in the way of temporary lighting devices and partitions. Eliminate the planned oak flooring and substitute carpeting because it's more flexible.

That word "flexible" recurs constantly in the communications from museum administrators. Every display, they explained, requires individual treatment, and the architectural space must be fully adaptable.

They were also concerned with natural light, which, in many exhibits, is either disturbing or harmful. Curators sought control of it. They also asked that the mirrors planned for both stairwells be taken out to make room for possible displays; in addition, the Sackler did not want pavilion light affected by the installation of stained glass. Then they criticized the balcony-like overlooks around the walls of the Great Hall. These, they felt, would be a security hazard, and would reduce vital wall space.

All of these changes were argued and undertaken after plans were approved and while construction was under way, and they shook the architectural team. Carlhian had planned every feature in question in order to carry out the basic requirement that the museums should attract and welcome their visitors, even luring them into the uneasy environment of sixty feet below ground. In a statement read to his critics, Carlhian pointed out that function sometimes "had to give way to the main concern of turning the visitors' underground trek into a pleasant journey." This involved the capturing of natural light and the "opening of vistas and perspectives."

"I strongly recommend," he wrote in a follow-up letter, "the retention of . . . window overlooks as allowing the opening of vistas considered essential to overcome the claustrophobic feelings of visitors in an underground facility."

Throughout his statements, Carlhian focused on visitors rather than on exhibits and their need for flexible treatment. His viewpoint indicated a conflict on the most basic terms with the museum administrators.

In the ancient profession of architecture, clients always get their way in the end. The architect hands over the key of the building, and what the user then does to the design is his business.

Here at the Smithsonian, however, the opening of the new underground museums had to coincide with the first exhibitions they would hold. So, before the design could be fulfilled, some of its splendor was subverted to the demands of the opening displays. Even the Great Hall, nucleus of the whole concept, keystone of the building's underground symmetry, was subdivided to raise the number of Sackler galleries to sixteen, all intimate enough to give full play to its small objects.

This was a grievous blow to the architectural team. Yet their product inevitably remains a treasure for the ages. The pavilions stand, externally the same, with their subtle motifs linking them to their quadrangle neighbors. And down below, the Great Hall is still all there, within the structure, ready to be restored when requirements change. Visitors yet to come may appreciate fully what a former Smithsonian executive described as the building's "descending vistas, superbly orchestrated."

In the long run, the old battle between the blueprints and the functions of a great building is seldom decided. Certainly no victor arises in this splendid structure. Like the ribs and strakes and gunwales of a new boat, the components here, human as well as mechanical, strain with tension.

But the thing floats. Superb collections reveal themselves within a superb architectural achievement. And the true triumph belongs to generations of Smithsonian visitors who will be enticed to enter, wonderingly, and who will leave profoundly enriched. ■

Owner	Smithsonian Institution
Construction administration	General Services Administration —National Capital Region
Architect	Shepley, Bulfinch, Richardson and Abbott
Landscaping	Landscape Architect of Record, Sasaki and Associates, Inc. Garden design and architectural features, SBRA Consultants: Lester Collins, Landscape Architect; James Buckler, Director of the Office of Horticulture, Smithsonian Institution
Engineers	
Structural	Ewell W. Finley, Inc.
Geotechnical	Mueser Rutledge Johnston and Desimone
Electrical and mechanical	Shooshanian Engineering Associates
General Contractor	Blake Construction Company
Consultants	
Lighting	Fisher Marantz
Mural artist	Richard Haas
Stained glass	Cummings Studios
Color	Tina Beebe
Acoustics	Lawrence G. Copley Associates
Security	Joseph M. Chapman, Inc.
Fire safety	Fire Pro Incorporated
Waterproofing	Simpson Gumpertz & Hegar, Inc.

Materials Sources

Masonry	
Limestone	Bybee Stone Co., Indiana
Granite	
Sunset Red	Texas Granite Company
Rockville Beige	Cold Spring Granite Company, Minn.
Columbia Pink	Rock of Ages, New Hampshire
Exposed metals	Polomyx—Systems Distributors, Inc.
Exposed wood	White oak
Flooring (Concourse)	Heatherbrown Wales—Shep Brown
Paint	Pittsburgh Paints
Special glazing (pavilions)	Triple Glaze—Economy Glass

Features

Foundation. Due to the lack of footings under the Castle and the A & I and their fragility, a slurry wall system was selected to minimize potential damage to historic landmarks.

Excavation. Resulting excavated area 285 ft by 430 ft—large enough to contain three Lincoln Memorials side by side.

Skylights. A pair of skylights, 117 ft long, bring natural light to exhibition galleries in both museums.

Four square skylights, 10 ft by 10 ft, bring natural light to the Concourse.

Glazed openings. Clear glass was selected throughout: in the pavilions' north windows, to allow untinted views of the garden and the Castle; in the Kiosk, to provide light penetration to the escalator vestibule. A layer of tinted glass is provided at the south window of each pavilion in order to minimize the impact of the Forrestal Building by day and offer visual excitement by night to Independence Avenue passers-by.

Dimensions

Site
Area, 4.2 acres. Distance from Freer Gallery to A & I, 540 ft; from Castle to Independence Ave, 350 ft. Openings between pavilions, 176 ft; between African and A & I, 82 ft to 90 ft; between Sackler and Freer, 92 ft; between A & I and Castle, 44 ft; between Kiosk and Castle, 44 ft; between Kiosk and Freer, 52 ft.

Buildings
Castle: length, 420 ft; A & I: length, 328 ft; Freer: length, 190 ft.

African Pavilion: length, 92 ft; width, 62 ft; height to top of cornice, 24 ft; height to top of domes, 36 ft.

Sackler Pavilion: length, 92 ft; width, 62 ft; height to top of cornice, 24 ft; height to top of pyramids, 38 ft.

Kiosk: width, 42 ft; height, 38 ft.

Interiors
Rotating gallery (Great Hall): width, 78 ft; length, 116 ft; height, 24 ft, 4 in; width, 27 ft.

Green Room: width, 27 ft; length, 42 ft.
Concourse: width, 27 ft; length, 240 ft; height, 42 ft.

Legend: B Bottom; C Center; L Left; R Right; T Top.

The following are abbreviations used to identify Smithsonian Institution bureaus and other sources.

SI Smithsonian Institution; OAHHP Office of Architectural History and Historic Preservation, SI; ODC Office of Design and Construction, SI; Freer, Freer Gallery of Art; Sackler, Arthur M. Sackler Gallery; NMAfA National Museum of African Art; EEA Eliot Elisofon Archives, NMAfA; SBRA Shepley, Bulfinch, Richardson and Abbott.

Front matter: pp. 2–3 Jean Paul Carlhian; 4–5 Robert C. Lautman; 8 SI; 14–15 Commercial Photographics, Washington, D.C.

Color: p. 31B courtesy of Office of Horticulture, SI; all other photographs by Robert C. Lautman.

A Special Place: pp. 34–35 SBRA; 36–37T Robert C. Lautman; 36–37B SBRA; 38 Robert C. Lautman; 39 SBRA.

Concepts: p. 40 Jeff Ploskonka, SI; 41 Jeff Tinsley, SI; 42L Richard Hofmeister, SI; 42R Jeff Tinsley, SI, courtesy Office of Folklife Programs; 43 Jeff Tinsley, SI, courtesy RAP; 44 Jeff Ploskonka, SI; 46–47 Richard B. Farrar, SI; 48T, 49T Kim Nielsen, courtesy Sackler; 48C reproduced from Robert Dale Owen, *Hints on Public Architecture*, De Capo Press, reprint 1978; 49B SBRA, courtesy ODC; 50L Ramiro A. Fernandez, courtesy, NMAfA; 50T Junzo Yoshimura, courtesy OAHHP; 51T Kim Nielsen, SI; 51B Junzo Yoshimura, courtesy OAHHP.

The Firm: p. 52 Bill Gallery; 53, 54L courtesy SBRA; 54B by permission of the Houghton Library, Harvard University, courtesy SBRA; 55–57 Bill Gallery.

The Architect: p. 58 Bill Gallery; 60–65 SBRA; 66 Robert C. Lautman; 67 Kim Nielsen.

Problems: p. 68 Bill Gallery; 70 reproduced by Bruce Reedy from the SI film *A New View from the Castle*; 71 courtesy Office of Horticulture, SI; 72L Robert C. Lautman; 72C Sasaki Associates, Inc.; 73 Richard Louie, courtesy Freer; 74TL and BL reproduced from Michele Pirazzoli-T'Serstevens, *Living Architecture: Chinese*, London: Macdonald, 1972; 74C Jean Paul Carlhian; 75T reproduced from Francisco Prieto-Moreno, *Los Jardines de Granada*, Madrid: Editorial Ciguena, 1952; 75B reproduced from Sylvia Crowe and Sheila Haywood, *The Gardens of Mughul India*, London: Thames and Hudson, 1972, photographs by Susan Jellico; 75C Jean Paul Carlhian; 76 Robert C. Lautman; 77T Commercial Photographics; 77B Robert C. Lautman; 78 Jean Paul Carlhian; 79R Richard Louie, courtesy Freer; 79L, SI; 80 SBRA; 81T reproduced from the General Services Administration, *Draft Environmental Impact Statement*, Washington, D.C., 1980; 81B SBRA.

Arthur M. Sackler Gallery: pp. 82–83 Arthur M. Sackler Collection, courtesy Sackler; 83B photograph by John Tsantes.

Architects at Work: pp. 84-88 Bill Gallery; 90 Kim Nielsen; 91–92L Bill Gallery; 92B drawing by Charles A. Platt, courtesy Freer; 93 SBRA, courtesy ODC; 94 Kim Nielsen; 95 Bill Gallery.

Solutions: p. 96 Robert C. Lautman; 97T SBRA, courtesy ODC; 98B Commercial Photographics; 99 Kim Nielsen, courtesy Sackler; 100–101 Jean Paul Carlhian; 103 Commercial Photographics; 104 Adolph Cluss and Schulze, courtesy SI Archives; 105L and C Robert C. Lautman; 105R Historic American Buildings Survey, Library of Congress; 106–7 Robert C. Lautman; 108 Kim Nielsen, courtesy Sackler; 109 Robert C. Lautman.

National Museum of African Art: pp. 110–11 courtesy NMAfA; 110R EEA; 111L photograph by Bruce Fleischer, EEA; 111C photograph by Kim Nielsen, EEA.

Landscape: p. 112 Robert C. Lautman; 114 James Renwick, Jr., courtesy OAHHP; 115L Library of Congress; 115R SI; 116 SI; 117L Richard B. Farrar, SI; 117R SI; 118TL Robert C. Lautman; 118–19 SBRA; 119BR–123 Robert C. Lautman.

The Big Hole: p. 124 Richard Louie, courtesy Freer; 125 Jeff Tinsley, SI; 126L Robert C. Lautman; 127 Richard Louie, courtesy Freer; 128 Commercial Photographics; 129L Richard Louie, courtesy Freer; 129R–131 Commercial Photographics; 132 Robert C. Lautman; 133 Jeff Ploskonka, SI.

Excellence: pp. 134, 136TL, TR, 137 Robert C. Lautman; 136C Kim Nielsen, courtesy Sackler; 138 Kim Nielsen, courtesy Sackler; 139 Robert C. Lautman; 140 Jeff Tinsley, SI; 141 SBRA, courtesy ODC; 142TL reproduced from Patrick Conner, *Oriental Architecture in the West*, London: Thames and Hudson, 1979, with permission of The Royal Pavilion, Art Gallery and Museums, Brighton; 142BL reproduced from Arnaldo Bruschi, *Bramante*, London: Thames and Hudson, 1977; 142C Jean Paul Carlhian; 143 Richard Louie, courtesy Freer; 144 Jeff Tinsley, SI; 145 Robert C. Lautman.

S. Dillon Ripley Center: p. 146TC SBRA; 146TL photograph by Polly Brown, courtesy Lucinda Leach, SITES; 146B photograph by Barbara S. Tuceling, courtesy SNAP; 147L Jeff Tinsley, SI, courtesy SITES; 147C Robert C. Lautman.

Satisfaction: pp. 148, 150B Robert C. Lautman; 151 Jean Paul Carlhian; 152–53 Albert Huang, SBRA.

Page 160, drawing by John Blake Murphy, courtesy OAHHP.

The Smithsonian Institution gratefully acknowledges the support of these donors who provided funds matching congressional appropriations for the construction of this building, which was dedicated September 28, 1987.

The Allbritton Foundation
The Boeing Company
The Coca-Cola Company
Dallah Establishment
Mr. and Mrs. Gaylord Donnelley
Mary Livingston Griggs and
   Mary Griggs Burke Foundation
Enid A. Haupt
H. J. Heinz II Charitable
   and Family Trust
The Hillman Foundation, Inc.
IBM Corporation
The Commemorative Association for
   the Japan World Exposition (1970)
The Government of Japan
The Japan Foundation
Mr. and Mrs. James M. Kemper, Jr.
Kettering Fund
The Republic of Korea

Kraft Foundation
Marriott Corporation
Brooks & Hope B. McCormick
   Foundation
NCR Foundation
Owens-Corning Fiberglas
   Corporation
Pew Memorial Trust
RJR Nabisco, Incorporated
Arthur M. and Jill Sackler
James Smithson Society
Smithsonian Associates
Mr. and Mrs. E. Hadley Stuart, Jr.
Elbridge & Mary Stuart Foundation
Mary Horner Stuart Foundation
The Ruth and Vernon Taylor Foundation
Texaco Philanthropic Foundation, Inc.
Wallace Funds

Alcoa Foundation
American Can Company Foundation
American Security Bank, N.A.
Mr. and Mrs. William S. Anderson
State of Bahrain
The Barra Foundation, Inc.
Mrs. Frederick C. Bartlett
Mr. and Mrs. Perry R. Bass
Henry C. Beck, Jr.
Mrs. Henry C. Beck, Jr.
Brown Group, Inc. Charitable Trust
Mr. and Mrs. Keith S. Brown
Burlington Northern Foundation
Citicorp/Citibank
Mr. and Mrs. David L. Coffin
Mr. and Mrs. James A. Elkins, Jr.
Roger S. Firestone Foundation

Folger Fund
Mr. and Mrs. Alfred C. Glassell, Jr.
Mr. and Mrs. John B. Greene
Mr. and Mrs. W. L. Hadley Griffin
GTE Foundation
Gordon Hanes
The Irwin Family
Japan Automobile Manufacturers' Association
Japan Electric Machine Industry Association
Japan Federation of Electric Power Companies
Japan Foreign Trade Council
Japan Iron & Steel Federation
Japanese Shipowners Association
The Mary Hillman Jennings Foundation
The Johnson Foundation (Trust)
Johnson's Wax Fund
King Ranch Family Trust

Seymour H. Knox Foundation, Inc.
Mr. and Mrs. LaRue Robbins Lutkins
Manufacturers Hanover Corporation
Merck and Company, Incorporated
Charles E. Merrill Trust
Dr. and Mrs. Ruben F. Mettler
Mobil Corporation
PACCAR Foundation
PepsiCo Foundation
Prince Charitable Trusts
Smith Richardson Foundation
The Riggs National Bank of Washington, D.C.
Mr. and Mrs. H. C. Seherr-Thoss
Standard Chartered Bank PLC
Tokyo Bankers' Association
Union Pacific Foundation